P9-DHF-304

IN LOVE WITH
QUILTS

LEISURE ARTS, INC.
and
OXMOOR HOUSE, INC.

EDITORIAL STAFF

Editor-in-Chief: Anne Van Wagner Childs
Executive Director: Sandra Graham Case
Executive Editor: Susan Frantz Wiles
Publications Director: Carla Bentley
Creative Art Director: Gloria Bearden
Production Art Director: Melinda Stout

PRODUCTION
Managing Editor: Susan White Sullivan
Senior Project Coordinator: Connie Irby
Project Coordinators: Mary Sullivan Hutcheson, Lisa Hinkle Lancaster, and Sherry Solida Ford

DESIGN
Design Director: Patricia Wallenfang Sowers
Senior Designer: Linda Diehl Tiano
Designers: Donna Waldrip Pittard, Diana Heien Suttle, and Rebecca Sunwall Werle

EDITORIAL
Associate Editor: Linda L. Trimble
Senior Editor: Laurie S. Rodwell
Senior Editorial Writer: Tammi Williamson-Bradley
Copy Editor: Laura Lee Stewart

ART
Book/Magazine Art Director: Diane Ghegan
Senior Production Artist: M. Katherine Yancey
Production Artists: Sarah J. Dearworth, Brent Jones, Larry Peyton, and Jennifer Isaacs Smith
Creative Art Assistant: Judith Howington Merritt
Photography Stylists: Karen Smart Hall, Christina Tiano, and Charlisa Erwin Parker
Typesetters: Cindy Lumpkin and Stephanie Cordero

ADVERTISING AND DIRECT MAIL
Copywriters: Steven M. Cooper, Marla Shivers, and Tena Kelley Vaughn
Designer: Rhonda H. Hestir
Art Director: Jeff Curtis
Production Artist: Linda Lovette Smart

BUSINESS STAFF

Publisher: Steve Patterson
Controller: Tom Siebenmorgen
Retail Sales Director: Richard Tignor
Retail Marketing Director: Pam Stebbins
Retail Customer Services Director: Margaret Sweetin

Marketing Manager: Russ Barnett
Executive Director of Marketing and Circulation: Guy A. Crossley
Fulfillment Manager: Byron L. Taylor
Print Production: Nancy Reddick Lister and Laura Lockhart

In Love With Quilts
from the *For the Love of Quilting* series
Published by Leisure Arts, Inc., and Oxmoor House, Inc.

Library of Congress Catalog Number: 93-85970
Hardcover ISBN 0-942237-25-0
Softcover ISBN 0-942237-26-9

INTRODUCTION

Patchwork quilts have a timeless appeal, and the same patterns that our great-grandmothers favored are just as pleasing in today's homes. Born out of necessity, quilts have become heirloom pieces that are treasured for their beauty and skillful handwork. American pioneer women often saved even the tiniest scraps of their precious fabrics, carefully arranging them to create intricate piecework designs. In a time when families kept personal belongings to a minimum, these artful creations were often a home's only adornments. We're proud to present **In Love With Quilts** as a tribute to American quilters. Along with several full-size versions of favorite old quilts, we've updated some traditional patterns and used them to create coordinating projects — such as pillows, wall hangings, and even decorated clothing — using quilting techniques. Whether you're an experienced quilter or just starting out, you'll love this treasury of keepsake quilts.

TABLE OF CONTENTS

BURGOYNE SURROUNDED 8
Burgoyne Surrounded Quilt.................................10

SAWTOOTH COLLECTION 14
Sawtooth Quilt 17
Throw 18

BASKET COLLECTION 24
Basket Quilt 27
Jumper and Hat...28

STAR OF THE ORIENT 32
Star of the Orient Quilt......................................34

NEIGHBORLY COLLECTION.....38

Schoolhouse Quilt..........................46
Hole in the Barn Door Table Rug..................47
Wall Hanging 48
Schoolhouse Pillow 49
Broken Dishes Pillow 49
Log Cabin Pillow 50
Hole in the Barn Door Pillow....................51

BABY QUILTS 54

Dresden Plate Quilt........................57
Bow Tie Quilt.............................58

CHURN DASH COLLECTION....60

Churn Dash Quilt..........................65
Churn Dash Apron 66
Table Runner 67
Potholder 68

QUILT BLOCK SAMPLER..........70

Quilt Block Sampler Wall Hanging..................72

NEW YORK BEAUTY 80
New York Beauty Quilt 82

BEAR'S PAW COLLECTION 86
Bear's Paw Quilt 90
Appliquéd Sweatshirt 91
Bear Overalls................................92
Wall Hanging 93

ALBUM QUILT 98
Album Quilt...............................100

SUNNY GARDEN...................102
Appliquéd Jacket..........................106
Appliquéd Shirt...........................106
Stuffed Blackbird 107
Sunflower Wall Hanging 107

MARINER'S COMPASS............ 112
Mariner's Compass Quilt.................................114

PINWHEEL QUILT................... 120
Pinwheel Quilt 122

COZY CHRISTMAS 124
Tree Skirt...129
Wall Hanging 130
Star Ornament 131
Tree Ornament 132
Snowman 132
Large Pillow 133
Small Pillow..133

PRETTY PILLOWS 138
Album Pillow 142
Bear's Paw Pillow 142
Bow Tie Pillow..142
Sawtooth Pillow...143
Churn Dash Pillow......................................143
Honey Bee Pillow.......................................144

GENERAL INSTRUCTIONS............................145
CREDITS 160

BURGOYNE SURROUNDED

In olden days, popular quilt patterns were often inspired by important events. The Burgoyne Surrounded design commemorates the surrender of British General John Burgoyne during the famous Revolutionary War battle at Saratoga in 1777. The blocks cleverly depict the Colonial troops surrounding the English infantry in a strategic maneuver that proved to be the turning point of the war. Although the design is traditionally pieced in red on a white background, the white-on-red combination shown here is a striking variation of this early favorite.

BURGOYNE SURROUNDED

Size
Block: 22″ x 22″
Quilt: 89″ x 89″

Yardage Requirements
White fabric — 2¼ yds of 45″w
Red fabric — 6¼ yds of 45″w
Binding — 1⅛ yds of 45″w white fabric
Backing — 7⅞ yds of 45″w **OR** 2⅝ yds of 108″w
120″ x 120″ piece of low-loft polyester bonded
   batting

Cutting Out Pieces
1. Follow **Making Templates**, pg. 147, to make
   templates from all patterns on pg. 12.
2. To complete our quilt you will need 16 blocks.
   Follow **Cutting Out Quilt Pieces**, pg. 147, and
   cut out the following:
   A — 848 from white fabric
   A — 704 from red fabric
   B — 128 from white fabric
   B — 192 from red fabric
   C — 128 from red fabric
   D — 64 from red fabric
   E — 64 from white fabric
   F — 64 (3½″ x 16½″) pieces from red fabric

Assembling The Quilt
1. For each block, follow **Piecing And Pressing**,
   pg. 148, and **Unit 1** diagram to sew pieces
   together to make **Unit 1**. Repeat to make a total
   of 2 **Unit 1's**.

Unit 1

2. Follow **Unit 2** diagram and sew pieces together
   to make **Unit 2**. Repeat to make a total of
   2 **Unit 2's**.

Unit 2

3. Follow **Unit 3** diagram and sew pieces together
   to make **Unit 3**.

Unit 3

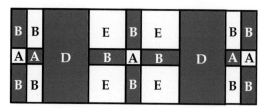

4. Follow **Unit 4** diagram and sew 2 **Unit 1's**,
   2 **Unit 2's**, and **Unit 3** together to make **Unit 4**.

Unit 4

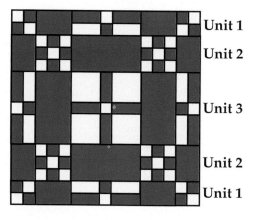

5. Follow **Unit 5** diagram and sew **Unit 4** between
   2 **F's** to make **Unit 5**.

Unit 5

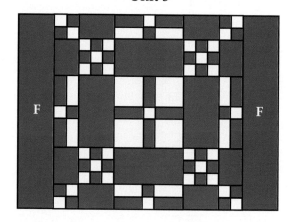

6. Follow **Unit 6** diagram and sew pieces together
   to make **Unit 6**. Repeat to make 2 **Unit 6's**.

Unit 6

7. Follow **Block** diagram and sew **Unit 5** between 2 **Unit 6's** to complete **Block**.

Block

8. Repeat to make 16 **Blocks**.
9. Sew 4 **Blocks** together to make **Row 1**. Repeat to make **Rows 2-4**.

Row 1

10. Match seamlines between blocks and sew **Row 1** to **Row 2**. Repeat to add **Rows 3** and **4** to complete **Quilt Top**.

Quilt Top

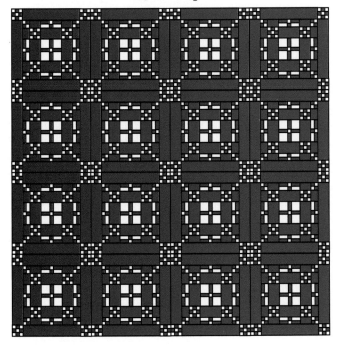

11. Follow **Marking Quilting Lines**, pg. 154, and **Quilting Diagram**, and **Quilting Patterns**, pg. 13, to mark quilting lines on quilt top, reversing pattern as necessary.

Quilting Diagram

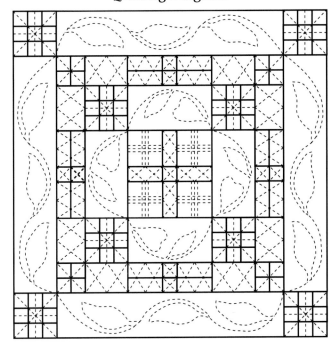

12. Follow **Preparing Backing And Batting**, pg. 155, to piece backing if necessary.
13. Follow **Assembling The Quilt**, pg. 155, to layer backing, batting, and quilt top and to baste all layers together.
14. Follow **Quilting**, pg. 156, and stitch quilt along marked lines. Trim batting and backing even with edges of quilt.
15. Follow **Making Continuous Bias Strip Binding**, pg. 156, and use a 36" square to make 10$\frac{1}{2}$ yds of 2$\frac{1}{2}$"w bias binding.
16. Follow **Attaching Binding With Mitered Corners**, pg. 157, and attach bias binding to quilt.

11

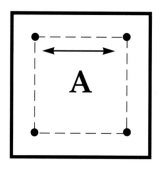

A

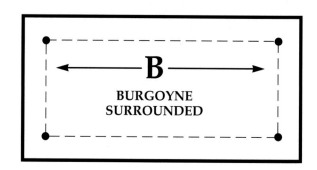

B

BURGOYNE
SURROUNDED

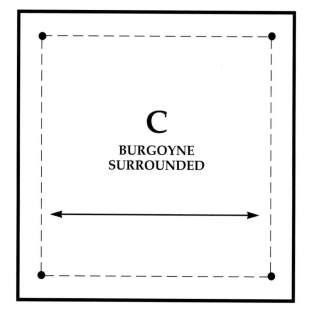

C

BURGOYNE
SURROUNDED

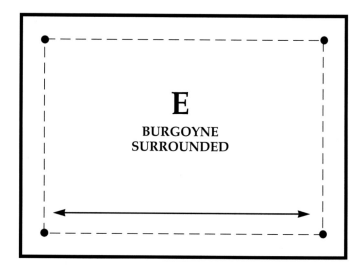

E

BURGOYNE
SURROUNDED

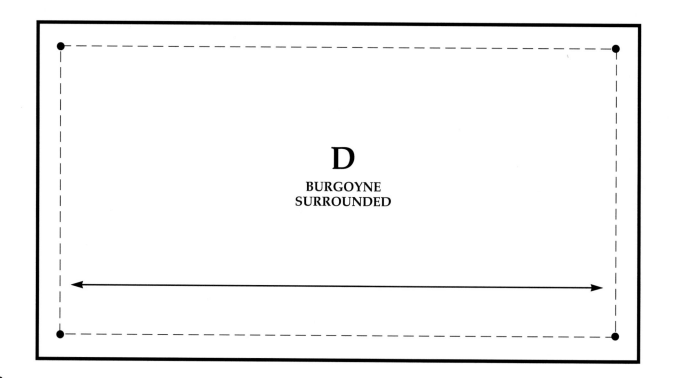

D

BURGOYNE
SURROUNDED

BURGOYNE SURROUNDED
QUILTING PATTERNS

SAWTOOTH COLLECTION

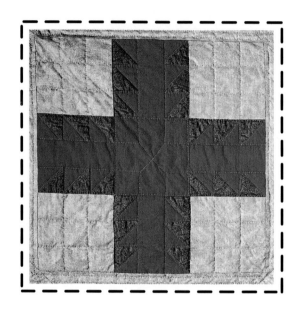

As families moved across the country or welcomed new people into their communities, quilt patterns were eagerly exchanged and often adapted to suit the stitchers' own tastes. The Sawtooth is a favorite that lent itself well to lots of variations. The quilt shown here features a sawtooth cross pattern alternated with beautifully quilted Snowball blocks. The more elaborate the quilting, the more likely that such a quilt was kept for use when special guests were entertained. Inspired by the softly colored terra-cotta fabric in this antique quilt, the throw on the following page reflects a Southwestern influence.

Vivid teal and rust teamed with a sandy-colored fabric create a sun-washed look on this eye-catching throw. Bright and colorful, the Indian-inspired quilt makes a cozy lap robe or decorative accent.

SAWTOOTH QUILT

Size
  Block: 10½" x 10½"
  Quilt: 77" x 77"

Yardage Requirements
  White fabric — 4⅞ yds of 45"w
  Tan fabric — 2¾ yds of 45"w
  Binding — ⅓ yd of 45"w
  Backing — 4¾ yds of 45"w OR 2⅜ yds of 90"w
  81" x 96" piece of low-loft polyester bonded
    batting

Cutting Out Pieces
1. Follow **Making Templates**, pg. 147, to make templates from patterns **A-H** on pgs. 20-21.
2. To complete our quilt, you will need 16 **Sawtooth Blocks**, 9 **Snowball Blocks**, and 12 **Half Blocks**. Follow **Cutting Out Quilt Pieces**, pg. 147, and cut out the following:
   Mitered Border — 4 (4½" x 81") pieces from white fabric
   A — 384 from white fabric
   A — 384 from tan fabric
   B — 64 from tan fabric
   C — 64 from white fabric
   C — 16 from tan fabric
   D — 48 from tan fabric
   E — 9 from white fabric
   F — 12 from white fabric
   G — 4 from white fabric
   H — 200 from white fabric
   H — 200 from tan fabric
   Binding — 4 (1" x 78") pieces

Assembling The Quilt
1. For each **Sawtooth Block**, follow **Piecing And Pressing**, pg. 148, and **Unit 1** diagram to sew pieces together to make **Unit 1**. Repeat to make a total of 4 **Unit 1's**.

Unit 1

2. Sew 1 **Unit 1** between 2 white **C's** to make **Unit 2**. Repeat to make a total of 2 **Unit 2's**. Sew 1 tan **C** between 2 **Unit 1's** to make **Unit 3**.

Unit 2   Unit 3

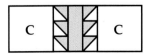   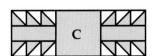

3. Follow **Sawtooth Block** diagram and sew **Unit 3** between 2 **Unit 2's** to complete **Sawtooth Block**.

Sawtooth Block

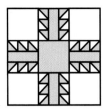

4. Repeat to make 16 **Blocks**.
5. For each **Snowball Block**, sew 4 **D's** to 1 **E**. Repeat to make 9 **Blocks**.

Snowball Block

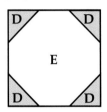

6. For each half block, sew 1 **D** to 1 **F**. Repeat to make 12 **Half Blocks**.

Half Block

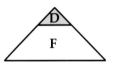

7. Follow **Assembly Diagram** to sew **Sawtooth Blocks**, **Snowball Blocks**, **Half Blocks**, and **G's** together.

Assembly Diagram

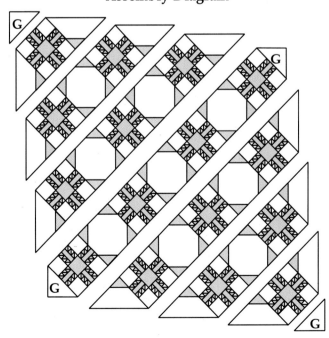

8. For top inner border, follow **Unit 4** diagram and sew 22 white **H's** to 22 tan **H's**. Repeat to make bottom border. For side inner border, sew 24 white **H's** to 24 tan **H's**. Repeat to make a total of 2 side borders. Follow **Unit 4** diagram to sew inner borders to top, bottom, and sides of assembled blocks.

Unit 4

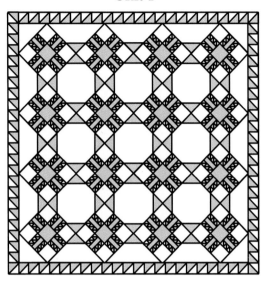

9. Follow **Adding Mitered Borders**, pg. 153, and add mitered borders to **Unit 4**.
10. For top outer border, follow **Quilt Top** diagram and sew 26 white **H's** to 26 tan **H's**. Repeat to make bottom border. For side outer border, sew 28 white **H's** to 28 tan **H's**. Repeat to make a total of 2 side borders. Follow **Quilt Top** diagram to sew outer borders to top, bottom, and sides of mitered borders to complete **Quilt Top**.

Quilt Top

11. Follow **Marking Quilting Lines**, pg. 154, **Quilting Diagram**, and **Quilting Pattern**, pg. 23, to mark quilting lines on quilt top.

Quilting Diagram

12. Follow **Preparing Backing And Batting**, pg. 155, to piece backing if necessary.
13. Follow **Assembling The Quilt**, pg. 155, to layer backing, batting, and quilt top and to baste all layers together.
14. Follow **Quilting**, pg. 156, and stitch quilt along marked lines. Trim batting and backing even with edges of quilt.
15. Press one long edge of each binding piece 1/4" to wrong side. Matching right sides and raw edges and using a 1/4" seam allowance, sew 1 piece of binding each to top and bottom of quilt. Trim short ends even with quilt. Fold binding over to quilt backing and pin pressed edge in place, covering stitching line. Blind stitch binding to backing.
16. With ends of binding extending 1/2" beyond quilt on each side, match right sides and raw edges and use a 1/4" seam allowance to sew 1 piece of binding to each side of quilt. Press short ends of binding 1/2" to wrong side. Fold binding over to quilt backing and pin pressed edge in place, covering stitching line. Blind stitch binding to backing.

THROW

Size
48" x 60"

Yardage Requirements
Tan fabric — 2 1/2 yds of 45"w
Rust fabric — 1 3/8 yds of 45"w
Teal fabric — 1/2 yd of 45"w
Binding fabric — 3/4 yds of 45"w
Backing fabric — 3 yds of 45"w **OR** 1 1/2 yds of 90"w
54" x 66" piece of fleece

Cutting Out Pieces

1. Follow **Making Templates**, pg. 147, to make templates from patterns **I-K** on pgs. 21-22.
2. Follow **Cutting Out Quilt Pieces**, pg. 147, and cut out the following:

   I — 88 from rust fabric
   I — 152 from teal fabric
   I — 192 from tan fabric
   J — 4 from rust fabric
   K — 4 from tan fabric
   K — 1 from rust fabric
   L — 2 (13$\frac{1}{2}$") squares from tan fabric, cut in half diagonally
   M — 2 (11$\frac{3}{4}$" x 26") pieces from tan fabric
   N — 2 (3$\frac{1}{2}$" x 48$\frac{1}{2}$") pieces from tan fabric
   O — 2 (4$\frac{1}{2}$" x 48$\frac{1}{2}$") pieces from rust fabric
   P — 2 (2$\frac{1}{2}$" x 48$\frac{1}{2}$") pieces from tan fabric

Assembling The Throw

1. Follow **Steps 1-3** of **Sawtooth Quilt** substituting patterns **I-K** for **A-C** to make 1 **Block**.
2. Follow **Unit 1** diagram to sew pieces to **Sawtooth Block** to make **Unit 1**.

Unit 1

3. Follow **Unit 2** diagram and sew 48 tan **I's**, 32 rust **I's**, and 16 teal **I's** together to make **Unit 2**. Repeat to make a total of 2 **Unit 2's**.

Unit 2

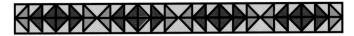

4. Follow **Unit 3** diagram and sew 24 tan **I's** and 24 teal **I's** together to make **Unit 3**. Repeat to make a total of 2 **Unit 3's**.

Unit 3

5. Follow **Unit 4** diagram and sew 24 tan **I's** and 24 teal **I's** together to make **Unit 4**. Repeat to make a total of 2 **Unit 4's**.

Unit 4

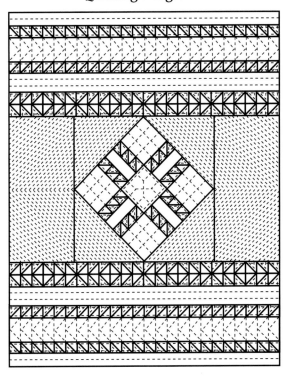

6. Follow **Throw Top** diagram to sew **Unit 1**, **Unit 2's**, **Unit 3's**, **Unit 4's**, **N's**, **O's**, and **P's** together to complete **Throw Top**.

Throw Top

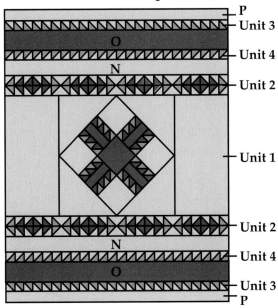

7. Follow **Marking Quilting Lines**, pg. 154, and **Quilting Diagram**, to mark quilting lines on throw top.

Quilting Diagram

8. Follow **Preparing Backing And Batting**, pg. 155, to piece backing if necessary.
9. Follow **Assembling The Quilt**, pg. 155, to layer backing, fleece, and throw top and to baste all layers together.

10. Follow **Quilting**, pg. 156, and stitch throw along marked lines. Trim batting and backing even with edges of throw.
11. Follow **Making Continuous Bias Strip Binding**, pg. 156, and use a 27" square to make 7 yds of 2¹/₂"w bias binding.
12. Follow **Attaching Binding With Mitered Corners**, pg. 157, to bind throw.

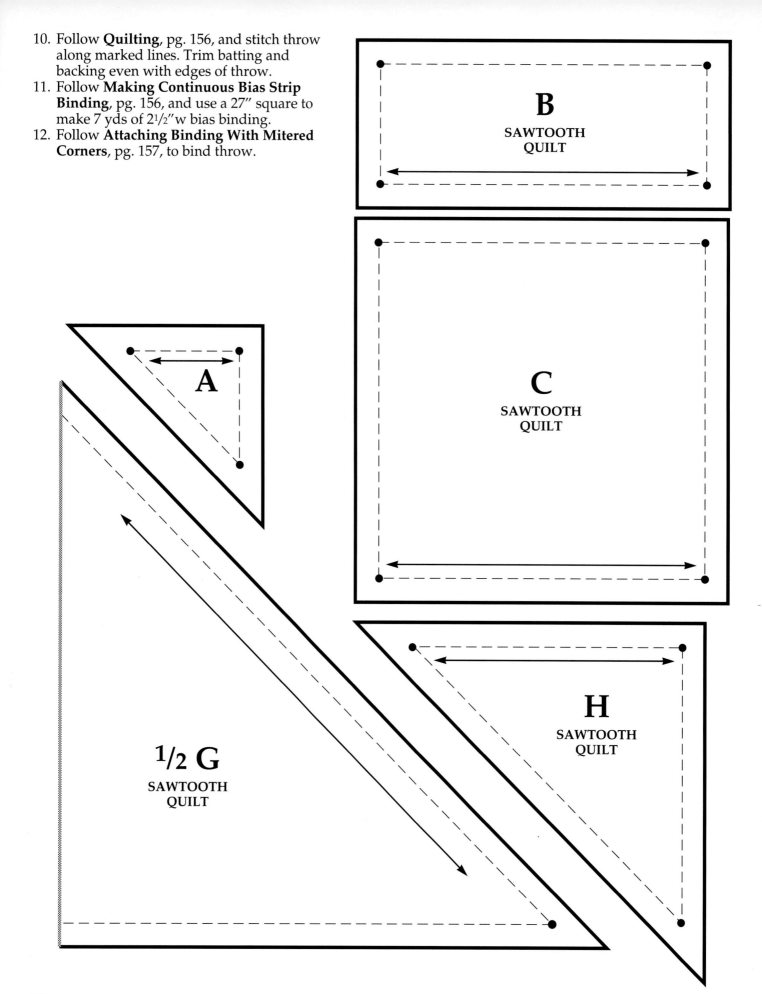

B
SAWTOOTH
QUILT

A

C
SAWTOOTH
QUILT

H
SAWTOOTH
QUILT

¹/₂ G
SAWTOOTH
QUILT

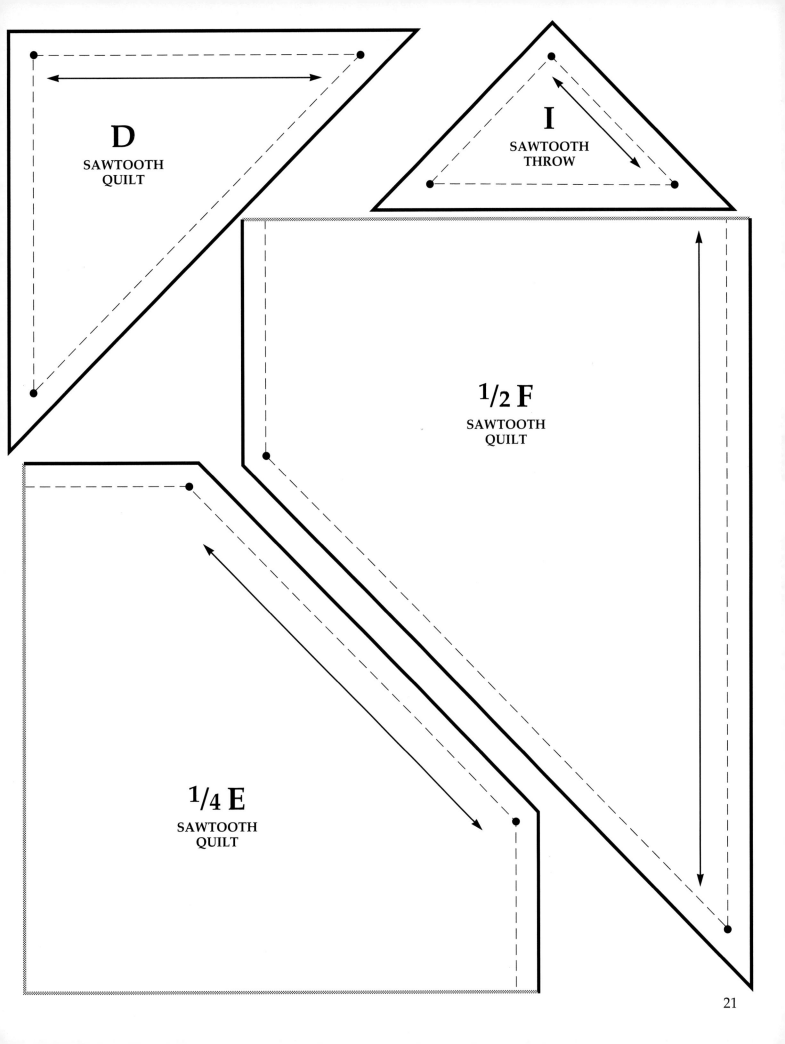

D
SAWTOOTH
QUILT

I
SAWTOOTH
THROW

½ F
SAWTOOTH
QUILT

¼ E
SAWTOOTH
QUILT

21

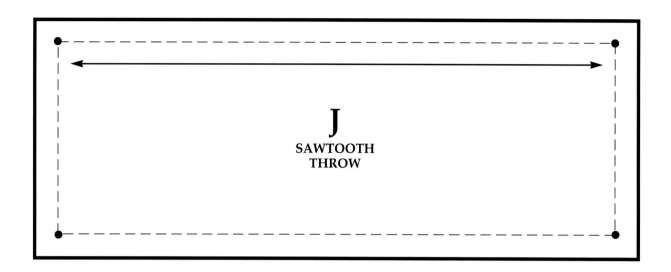

J
SAWTOOTH
THROW

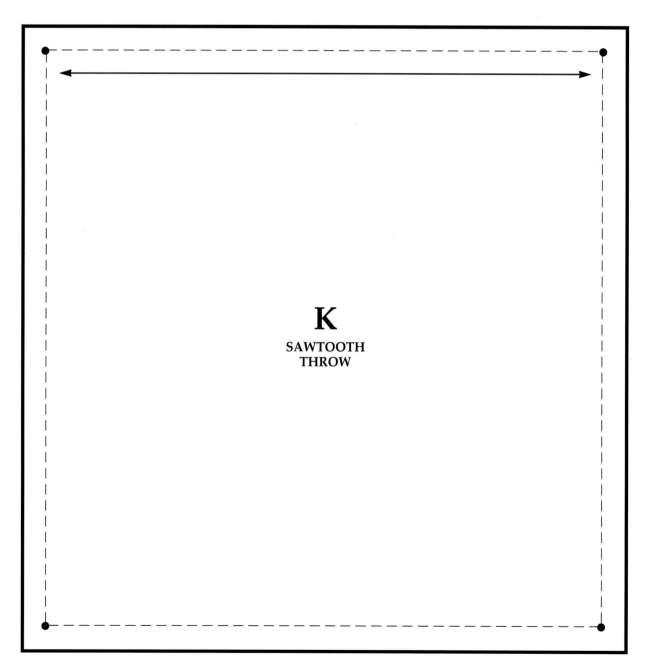

K
SAWTOOTH
THROW

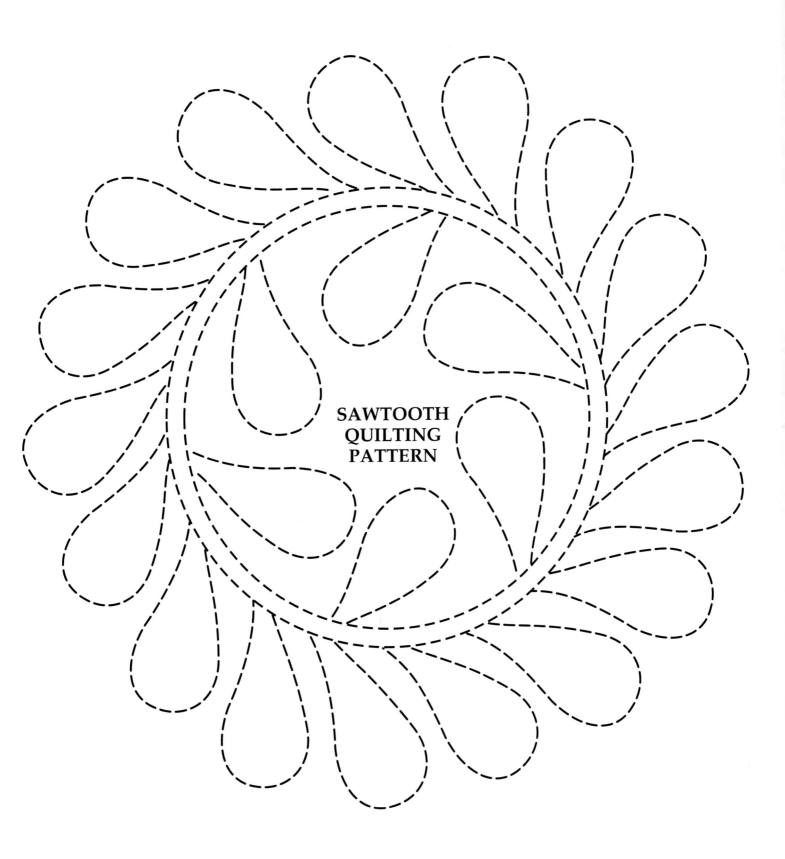

SAWTOOTH
QUILTING
PATTERN

BASKET COLLECTION

Back *when our grandmothers were little girls, baskets played an important role in everyday life. They were used for everything from gathering eggs to picking flowers or storing needle and thread — perhaps even to hold a little girl's doll clothes. Because such familiar images often inspired a quilter's creations, it was only natural that the basket would be a popular subject. In fact, no quilt collection of the day would have been complete without at least one Basket quilt. The feminine pattern was a favorite of little girls, but it was equally loved by women of all ages. Then, as now, blue and white was a prized color combination for delicate quilt patterns such as the one shown here.*

Enhancing our lives today, baskets are charming reminders of the simplicity of yesteryear. Perfect for a picnic in the country, this denim jumper features an appliquéd basket overflowing with old-fashioned Yo-Yo flowers. The matching hat, trimmed with more Yo-Yo flowers, lace, and ribbons, will shade your eyes from the sun.

BASKET QUILT

Size
Block: 9" x 9"
Quilt: 64" x 77"

Yardage Requirements
Ecru fabric — 2½ yds of 45"w
Blue dot fabric for blocks — 1⅝ yds of 45"w
Blue print fabric for sashing and borders —
   2⅜ yds of 45"w
Binding — ¾ yd of 45"w ecru fabric
Backing — 5 yds of 45"w **OR** 2¼ yds of 90"w
72" x 90" piece of low-loft polyester bonded
   batting

Cutting Out Pieces
1. Follow **Making Templates**, pg. 147, to make templates from patterns **A-F** on pgs. 30-31. (*Note: Pattern for appliqué template E does not include seam allowance; add seam allowance when pieces are cut out.*)
2. To complete our quilt you will need 30 blocks. Follow **Cutting Out Quilt Pieces**, pg. 147, and cut out the following:
   Sashing — 25 (3¾" x 9½") pieces from blue print fabric
   Sashing — 6 (3¾" x 70¾") pieces from blue print fabric
   Borders — 2 (3¾" x 65") pieces from blue print fabric
   A — 180 from ecru fabric
   A — 270 from blue dot fabric
   B — 60 from ecru fabric
   C — 30 from blue dot fabric
   D — 30 from ecru fabric
   E — 30 from blue dot fabric
   F — 30 from ecru fabric

Assembling The Quilt
1. For each block, follow **Piecing And Pressing**, pg. 148, and **Unit 1** diagram to sew pieces together to make **Unit 1**.

Unit 1
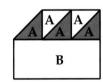

2. Follow **Unit 2** diagram and sew pieces together to make **Unit 2**.

Unit 2

3. Sew **Unit 1** to **Unit 2** to make **Unit 3**.

Unit 3
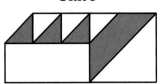

4. Follow **Unit 4** diagram and sew pieces together to make **Unit 4**.

Unit 4
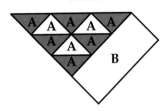

5. Sew **Unit 3** to **Unit 4** to make **Unit 5**.

Unit 5
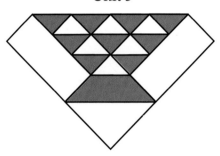

6. Follow **Hand Appliqué**, pg. 151, and appliqué **E** to **F** to make **Unit 6**.

Unit 6
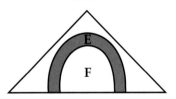

7. Sew **Unit 5** to **Unit 6** to complete **Block**.

Block

8. Repeat to make 30 **Blocks**.
9. Sew 5 (9½") sashing strips between 6 **Blocks** to make **Row 1**. Repeat to make **Rows 2-5**. Sew **Row 1** between 2 (70¾") sashing strips. Repeat to add **Rows 2-5** and remaining 70¾" sashing strips to make **Unit 7**.

Row 1   **Unit 7**

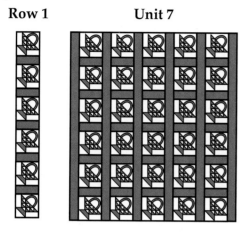

10. Sew 1 (65") sashing strip each to top and bottom of **Unit 7** to complete **Quilt Top**.

Quilt Top

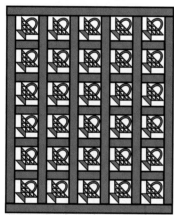

11. Follow **Marking Quilting Lines**, pg. 154, and **Quilting Diagram** and **Quilting Patterns**, pg. 31, to mark quilting lines on quilt top.

Quilting Diagram

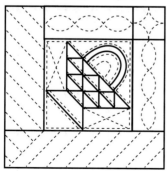

12. Follow **Preparing Backing And Batting**, pg. 155, to piece backing if necessary.
13. Follow **Assembling The Quilt**, pg. 155, to layer backing, batting, and quilt top and baste all layers together.
14. Follow **Quilting**, pg. 156, and stitch quilt along marked lines. Trim batting and backing even with edges of quilt.
15. Follow **Making Continuous Bias Strip Binding**, pg. 156, and use a 27" square to make 8½ yds of 1½"w bias binding.
16. Follow **Attaching Binding With Mitered Corners**, pg. 157, and attach bias binding to quilt.

JUMPER & HAT

Supplies For Jumper
Denim jumper
¼ yd — 45"w fabric for basket appliqué
11 (5") squares of assorted print fabrics for yo-yo flowers
⅞ yd — 45"w fabric for bias binding
3 yds — ¼"w flat cotton lace
1 (6") square doily with Battenberg lace trim
1½ yds — ⅜"w satin ribbon for leaves
8 assorted buttons for flower centers
Thread to match
Compass

Supplies For Hat
Denim hat
6 (5") squares of assorted print fabrics for yo-yo flowers
2⅛ yds — ¼"w flat cotton lace
1 (6") square doily with Battenberg lace trim
1 yd — ⅜"w satin ribbon for leaves
½ yd — ⅝"w satin ribbon
6 assorted buttons for flower centers
Thread to match
Glue gun and glue sticks
Thick, clear-drying craft glue
Compass

Making The Jumper
1. Wash, dry, and press jumper, fabrics, doily, lace, and ribbon.
2. For bias binding, measure neck and each armhole edge. Cut 3 bias strips of fabric 3½" wide by the determined measurements plus 1".
3. Matching wrong sides and long raw edges, fold binding in half; press. Press one short raw edge of each binding piece ½" to wrong side. Match right side and raw edges of binding to wrong side of neck and armhole edges of jumper, placing folded end of binding at a seam. Sew binding to jumper using a ¼" seam allowance.

4. Press binding to right side of jumper. Place straight edge of lace under folded edge of binding; topstitch binding and lace to jumper along folded edge of binding *(Fig. 1)*.

Fig. 1

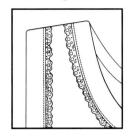

5. Follow **Making Templates**, pg. 147, to make templates from appliqué patterns **G** and **H** on pgs. 30-31. Cut out the following:
   G — 1 from basket fabric
   H — 1 from basket fabric
   I — 3 (3") squares from basket fabric
   J — 1 (1" x 9") piece from basket fabric
6. Refer to **Hand Appliqué**, pg. 151, to appliqué **G** to front of jumper.
7. Cut doily as shown in **Fig. 2**. Discard smaller piece of doily.

Fig. 2

8. Fold 1 **I** in half diagonally; press. Fold in half again and press to make prairie point. Repeat to make a total of 3 prairie points. Matching raw edges, pin prairie points to right side of doily *(Fig. 3)*.

Fig. 3

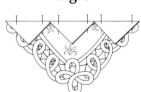

9. Press 1 long raw edge of **J** 1/4" to wrong side. Matching right sides and raw edges, pin and sew unpressed edge of **J** to prairie points and doily using a 1/4" seam allowance. Press seam toward **J**. Press short ends to wrong side at end of doily. Covering raw edges of handle, topstitch doily to jumper along both long edges of **J**.

10. Refer to photo for placement and hand appliqué **H** to jumper.
11. Sew edge of doily to jumper leaving Battenberg lace free.
12. To make yo-yo flowers, cut 4 (4") circles and 4 (3") circles from assorted fabrics. Turn raw edges under 1/4" and baste close to edge. Pull basting thread to gather circle as tightly as possible; knot and clip ends of thread. Gathered side of flower is front.
13. To make buds, cut 3 (2 1/2") circles from assorted fabrics. Fold 1 circle in half; then turn folded edge to center. Baste 1/4" from raw edges *(Fig. 4)*. Pull basting thread to gather bud as tightly as possible; knot and clip ends of thread. Wrap raw edges with 4" length of ribbon; hand stitch in place. Repeat to make a total of 3 buds.

Fig. 4

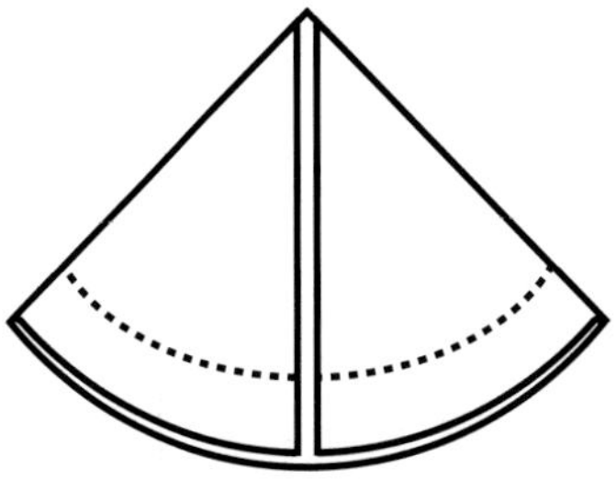

14. To make leaves, cut 10 (3 1/2") lengths of ribbon. With 1 length of ribbon, make a loop with right side of ribbon up *(Fig. 5)*; press loop down to make a point. Repeat to make a total of 10 leaves.

Fig. 5

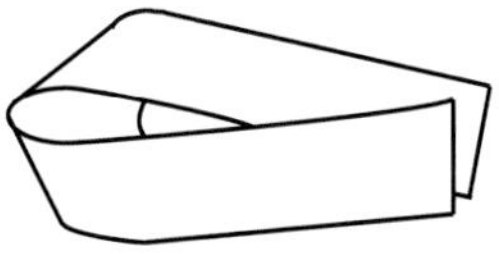

15. Refer to photo and sew leaves and buds to backs of flowers. Position each flower on jumper; place button in center of flower and sew to jumper through button.

Making The Hat

1. Refer to photo and use thick, clear-drying craft glue to glue the 1/4"w lace to both sides of brim of hat. Allow glue to dry.
2. Trim away fabric center of doily, leaving Battenberg lace. Baste around inside edge of lace. Pull basting thread to loosely gather lace; knot and clip ends of thread.
3. Cut 2 (8") lengths of 5/8"w ribbon. With 1 length of ribbon, make a loop with right side of ribbon up *(Fig. 5, pg. 29)*; press loop down to make a point. Repeat to make a total of 2 loops.
4. Refer to photo and hot glue ribbon loops to hat. Hot glue gathered lace to hat on top of ribbon.
5. Cut 4 (4") circles and 2 (3") circles from assorted fabrics and follow **Step 12** of **Making The Jumper**, pg. 29, to make yo-yo flowers. Sew buttons to centers of flowers.
6. Follow **Step 14** of **Making The Jumper** to make 11 leaves.
7. Refer to photo and hot glue leaves and flowers to hat.

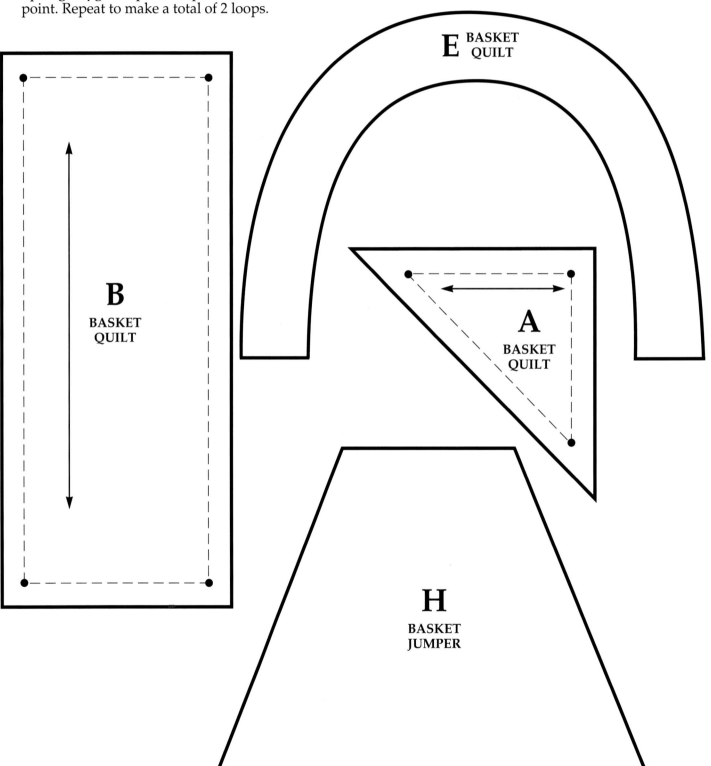

E BASKET QUILT

B BASKET QUILT

A BASKET QUILT

H BASKET JUMPER

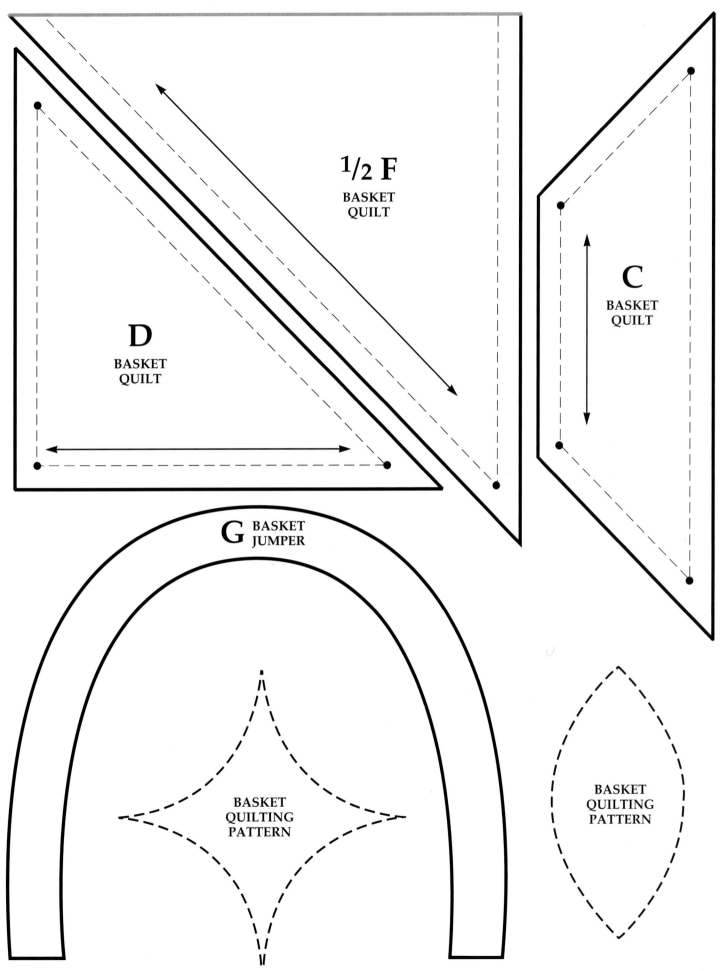

$^1/_2$ **F**
BASKET QUILT

D
BASKET QUILT

C
BASKET QUILT

G BASKET JUMPER

BASKET QUILTING PATTERN

BASKET QUILTING PATTERN

31

STAR OF THE ORIENT

Providing an exciting challenge for the experienced quilter, the Star of the Orient is a lovely contemporary design with its roots in traditional favorites. The intricate pattern features eight-pointed stars that are created with interlocking pieces of fabric and framed with Pineapple borders. Pictured here, a variety of fabrics with small prints gives this modern quilt a charmingly old-fashioned look.

STAR OF THE ORIENT

Size
Block: 14" x 14"
Quilt: 84" x 98"

Yardage Requirements
White fabric — 2¾ yds of 45"w
Assorted light pink fabrics — ¾ yd of 45"w
Assorted dark pink fabrics — 1 yd of 45"w
Assorted light orange fabrics — 1⅛ yds of 45"w
Assorted dark orange fabrics — ⅝ yd of 45"w
Assorted light yellow fabrics — 1⅛ yds of 45"w
Assorted dark yellow fabrics — ⅝ yd of 45"w
Assorted light green fabrics — 1⅛ yds of 45"w
Assorted dark green fabrics — 1 yd of 45"w
Assorted light blue fabrics — ⅜ yd of 45"w
Assorted dark blue fabrics — 1 yd of 45"w
Assorted light purple fabrics — ⅜ yd of 45"w
Assorted dark purple fabrics — ½ yd of 45"w
Assorted grey fabrics — ⅜ yd of 45"w
Binding — 1⅛ yds of 45"w
Backing — 6 yds of 45"w **OR** 2½ yds of 108"w
90" x 108" piece of low-loft polyester bonded
    batting

Cutting Out Pieces
1. Follow **Making Templates**, pg. 147, to make
   templates from all patterns on pgs. 36-37.
2. To complete our quilt you will need 42 blocks.
   Before cutting out pieces, look at the quilt photo
   and diagrams. You'll notice that for each
   individual block you will need to cut the **B** and **C**
   pieces from the same fabric for each set of colors.
   For example, for each individual block you will
   need 1 **B** and 1 **C** cut from the same dark pink
   fabric, 1 **B** and 1 **C** cut from the same light orange
   fabric, etc. Also, for pieces **D-I**, you will need 4
   matching pieces for each block. For example, for
   each individual block you will need 4 **D's** cut from
   the same dark blue fabric, 4 **E's** cut from the
   same light green fabric, etc. Follow **Cutting Out Quilt
   Pieces**, pg. 147, and cut out the following:
   A — 42 from white fabric
   B — 42 from each of the assorted colors of dark
        pinks, light oranges, light yellows, greys, light
        greens, dark greens, light blues, and light purples
   C — 42 from each of the assorted colors of dark
        pinks, light oranges, light yellows, greys, light
        greens, dark greens, light blues, and light
        purples (1 to match each **B**)
   C — 336 from white fabric
   D — 84 from dark purple fabrics (cut in sets of 4)
   D — 84 from dark blue fabrics (cut in sets of 4)
   E — 84 from light pink fabrics (cut in sets of 4)
   E — 84 from light green fabrics (cut in sets of 4)
   F — 84 from dark pink fabrics (cut in sets of 4)
   F — 84 from dark green fabrics (cut in sets of 4)
   G — 84 from light orange fabrics (cut in sets of 4)
   G — 84 from light yellow fabrics (cut in sets of 4)

H — 84 from dark orange fabrics (cut in sets of 4)
H — 84 from dark yellow fabrics (cut in sets of 4)
I — 84 from white fabric
I — 84 from dark blue fabrics (cut in sets of 4)

Assembling The Quilt
1. For each block, follow **Piecing And Pressing**,
   pg. 148, and sew dark pink **B** to **A halfway** down
   1 side of the octagon *(Fig. 1)*.

Fig. 1

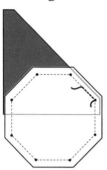

2. Sew 1 light purple **B** to dark pink **B** and **A** as
   shown in **Fig. 2**. Referring to **Unit 1** diagram for
   color placement, continue adding **B's** in a
   counterclockwise direction, completing first seam
   when adding last **B** to make **Unit 1**.

Fig. 2   **Unit 1**

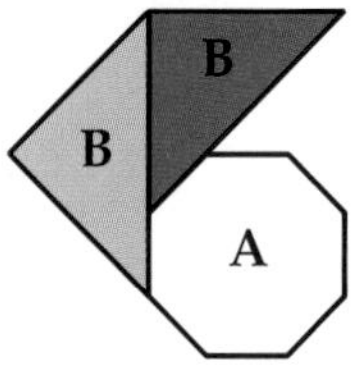

3. Using **C** fabrics to match **B** fabrics, sew 1 white **C**
   to 1 colored **C** to make **Unit 2**. Repeat to make a
   total of 8 **Unit 2's**.

Unit 2

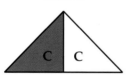

4. Referring to **Fig. 3** for color placement, sew dark
   pink **Unit 2** to **Unit 1 halfway** down 1 side of the
   octagon *(Fig. 3)*.

Fig. 3

34

5. Referring to **Unit 3** diagram for color placement, continue adding **Unit 2's** in a counterclockwise direction, completing first seam when adding last **Unit 2** to make **Unit 3**.

Unit 3

6. Repeat **Steps 1-5** to make 42 **Unit 3's**.
7. Referring to **Block #1** and **Block #2** diagrams for color placement, sew pieces **D-I** to **Unit 3's** in alphabetical order. Repeat to make 21 **Block #1's** and 21 **Block #2's**.

Block #1

Block #2

8. Sew 3 **Block #1's** and 3 **Block #2's** together to make **Row 1**. Repeat to make **Rows 2-7**.

Row 1

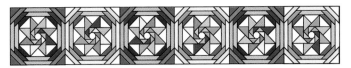

9. Referring to **Quilt Top** diagram for placement, sew **Rows 1-7** together to complete **Quilt Top**.

Quilt Top

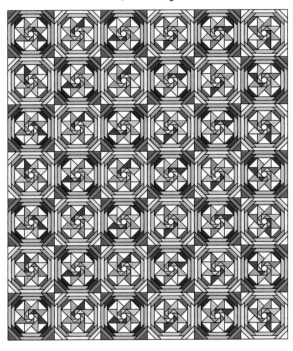

10. Follow **Preparing Backing And Batting**, pg. 155, to piece backing if necessary.
11. Follow **Assembling The Quilt**, pg. 155, to layer backing, batting, and quilt top and to baste all layers together.
12. Follow **Quilting**, pg. 156, and stitch quilt in the ditch along all seamlines. Trim batting and backing even with edges of quilt.
13. Follow **Making Continuous Bias Strip Binding**, pg. 156, and use a 36" square to make 11 yds of 2"w bias binding.
14. Follow **Attaching Binding With Mitered Corners**, pg. 157, and attach bias binding to quilt.

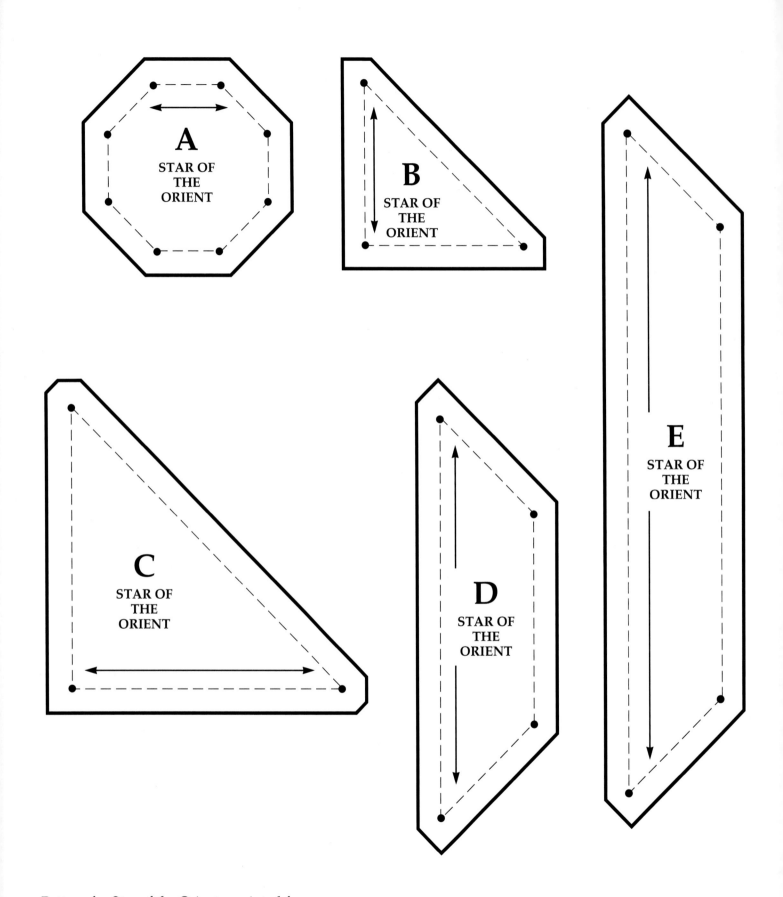

Pattern for Star of the Orient reprinted from
Scrap Quilts by Judy Martin, with permission from
Leman Publications, Inc.

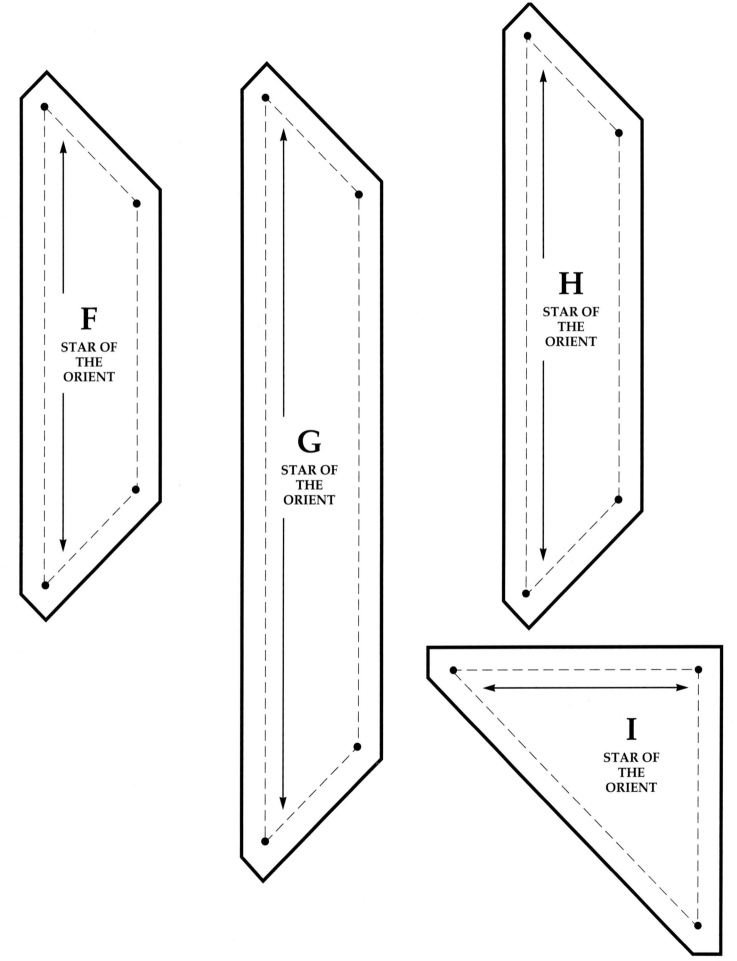

F
STAR OF
THE
ORIENT

G
STAR OF
THE
ORIENT

H
STAR OF
THE
ORIENT

I
STAR OF
THE
ORIENT

NEIGHBORLY COLLECTION

Early quilters contributed much to the growth of American folk art, creating unique designs using their own variations and combinations of popular patterns. Their artistic legacy of imaginative quilts still inspires us today. The quilt shown here, sewn during the last century by a woman unknown to us now, may have been a scrap quilt pieced from blocks left over from other quilts. Or perhaps the scattered Schoolhouse blocks represented her town, with the plain strips depicting the fields and pathways between the homes. A closer look reveals that one of the houses is upside down! Was this a mistake — or did the house belong to an unconventional member of the community (maybe even the quilter herself)? We may never know about the life of this quilter of old, but we can be sure she never imagined that her work would appear in a quilting book a hundred years later! Inspired by her handiwork, we've provided patterns and instructions for making a traditional Schoolhouse quilt, along with a host of coordinating projects to spark your own creativity.

Created with simple shapes and a variety of fabrics, this appliquéd wall quilt will add a homey touch to any room. A bright red road connects the houses in the neighborly little village, and stylized trees dot the countryside. Scraps of red and blue fabric provide a lively contrast to the neutral color scheme.

An inviting pillow makes any chair a cozy spot to relax and enjoy a snack. Adding a splash of color, the charming table rug below features an old country pattern known as Hole in the Barn Door.

(Opposite) First popular in the late 1800's, the traditional Schoolhouse quilt pattern was a symbol of a frontier community's stability and respectability. The quilt shown here reflects that old-fashioned spirit of neighborliness.

(Pages 44-45) These pillows were inspired by the colors and patterns of the folk art quilt shown on page 39. The collection includes two Log Cabin block pillows, one Schoolhouse, one Hole in the Barn Door, and two pillows featuring Broken Dishes blocks.

SCHOOLHOUSE QUILT

Size
Block: 9" x 9"
Quilt: 65" x 86"

Yardage Requirements
Ecru fabric — 2 yds of 45"w
Assorted fabrics — total of 3½ yds of 45"w
Black fabric for setting squares — ³/₈ yd of 45"w
Blue fabric for sashing — 1 yd of 45"w
Tan fabric for sashing — ⁵/₈ yd of 45"w
Rust fabric for sashing — ⁵/₈ yd of 45"w
Binding — ³/₄ yd of 45"w
Backing — 5 yds of 45"w **OR** 2½ yds of 90"w
81" x 96" piece of low-loft polyester bonded
　batting

Cutting Out Pieces
1. Follow **Making Templates**, pg. 147, to make
　templates from patterns **A-O** on pgs. 51-53.
2. To complete our quilt, you will need 48 blocks.
　Follow Cutting Out Quilt Pieces, pg. 147, and
　cut out the following:
　A — 96 from ecru fabric
　B — 96 from assorted fabrics
　C — 48 from ecru fabric
　D — 48 from ecru fabric
　D (reversed) — 48 from ecru fabric
　E — 48 from assorted fabrics
　F — 48 from ecru fabric
　G — 48 from assorted fabrics
　H — 96 from assorted fabrics
　I — 48 from assorted fabrics
　J — 48 from assorted fabrics
　K — 48 from ecru fabric
　L — 144 from assorted fabrics
　M — 96 from assorted fabrics
　N — 96 from assorted fabrics
　O — 48 from ecru fabric
　P — 54 (1¼" x 9½") pieces from tan fabric
　P — 54 (1¼" x 9½") pieces from rust fabric
　Sashing — 56 (2" x 9½") pieces from blue fabric
　Setting squares — 63 (2") squares from black
　　fabric

Assembling The Quilt
1. For each block, follow **Piecing And Pressing**,
　pg. 148, and **Unit 1** diagram to sew pieces
　together to make **Unit 1**.

Unit 1

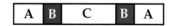

2. Follow **Unit 2** diagram to sew pieces together to
　make **Unit 2**.

Unit 2

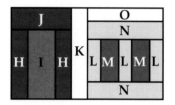

3. Follow **Unit 3** diagram to sew pieces together to
　make **Unit 3**, sewing pieces **H-K** together and
　L-O together before joining the sections.

Unit 3

4. Sew **Unit 1, Unit 2,** and **Unit 3** together to
　complete **Block**.

Block

5. Repeat **Steps 1-4** to make 48 **Blocks**.
6. Sew 6 **Blocks** between 7 sashing strips to make
　Row 1. Repeat to make **Rows 2-8**.

Row 1

7. Sew 1 tan **P** to 1 rust **P** to make **Unit 4**. Repeat to
　make a total of 54 **Unit 4's**.

Unit 4

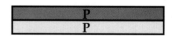

8. Sew 6 **Unit 4's** between 7 setting squares to
　make **Unit 5**. Repeat to make a total of
　9 **Unit 5's**.

Unit 5

9. Sew **Row 1** between 2 **Unit 5's**. Repeat to add **Rows 2-8** and remaining **Unit 5's** to complete **Quilt Top**.

Quilt Top

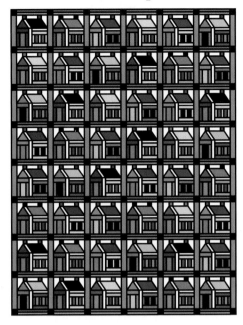

10. Follow **Preparing Backing And Batting**, pg. 155, to piece backing if necessary.
11. Follow **Assembling The Quilt**, pg. 155, to layer backing, batting, and quilt top, and to baste all layers together.
12. Follow **Quilting**, pg. 156, and stitch quilt in the ditch along all seamlines. Trim batting and backing even with edges of quilt.
13. Follow **Making Continuous Bias Strip Binding**, pg. 156, and use a 27" square to make 9 yds of 2½"w binding.
14. Follow **Attaching Binding With Mitered Corners**, pg. 157, and attach bias binding to quilt.

HOLE IN THE BARN DOOR TABLE RUG

Size
Block: 11" x 9"
Rug: 32" x 26"

Yardage Requirements
Assorted light fabrics — total of ½ yd of 45"w
Assorted medium fabrics — total of 1 yd of 45"w
Assorted dark fabrics — total of ½ yd of 45"w
Medium fabrics for sashing — ⅝ yd of 45"w
Setting blocks — ¼ yd of 45"w
Binding — ½ yd of 45"w
Backing — 1¼ yds of 45"w
Fleece — ⅞ yd of 45"w

Cutting Out Pieces
1. Follow **Making Templates**, pg. 147, to make template from pattern **Q** on pg. 52.
2. To complete our table rug, you will need 4 blocks. Follow **Cutting Out Quilt Pieces**, pg. 147, and cut out the following:
   Q — 16 from light fabrics
   Q — 16 from dark fabrics
   R — 16 (3" x 1⅞") pieces from dark fabrics
   S — 4 (3") squares from light fabrics
   T — 16 (1⅞" x 5¾") pieces from medium fabrics
   U — 16 (1⅞") squares from medium fabrics
   V — 4 (1" x 8½") pieces from light fabrics
   W — 4 (1¼" x 8⅞") pieces from light fabrics
   X — 4 (1⅛" x 9¼") pieces from dark fabrics
   Y — 4 (2¾" x 9½") pieces from medium fabrics
   Z — 8 (2½" x 11½") pieces from medium fabrics
   AA — 4 (2¼" x 9½") pieces from medium fabrics
   Sashing — 4 (4" x 9½") pieces from medium fabric
   Setting blocks — 12 (2½" x 4") pieces
   Binding — 2 (2½" x 27") and 2 (2½" x 34") pieces

Assembling The Table Rug
1. For each block, follow **Piecing And Pressing**, pg. 148, and **Unit 1** diagram to sew pieces together to make **Unit 1**. Follow **Unit 2** diagram and sew pieces together to make **Unit 2**.

Unit 1   **Unit 2**

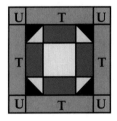

2. Follow **Block** diagram and sew pieces to **Unit 2** in alphabetical order to complete **Block**.

Block

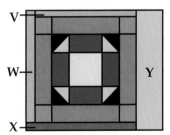

3. Repeat **Steps 1-2** to make 4 **Blocks**.

4. Sew 2 medium **Z's** between 3 setting blocks to make **Row 1**. Repeat to make **Rows 3, 4,** and **6**.

Row 1

5. Sew 2 **Blocks** between 2 sashing strips and 2 **AA's** to make **Row 2**. Repeat to make **Row 5**.

Row 2

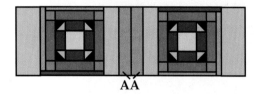

AA

6. Sew **Rows 1-6** together to complete **Table Rug Top**.

Table Rug Top

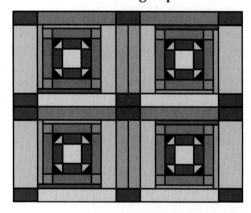

7. Follow **Assembling The Quilt**, pg. 155, to layer backing, fleece, and table rug top and to baste all layers together.
8. Follow **Quilting**, pg. 156, and stitch table rug in the ditch along all seamlines. Trim fleece and backing even with edges of table rug.
9. Press one long edge of each binding piece 1/4" to wrong side.
10. Matching right sides and raw edges and using a 1/4" seam allowance, sew 1 (34") binding piece to top and bottom of table rug. Trim short ends even with table rug. Fold binding over to table rug backing and pin pressed edge in place covering stitching line. Blind stitch binding to backing.
11. With ends of binding extending 1/2" beyond table rug on each side, match right sides and raw edges and use a 1/4" seam allowance to sew one 27" piece of binding to each side of table rug. Press short ends of binding 1/2" to wrong side. Fold binding over to table rug backing and pin pressed edge in place covering stitching line. Blind stitch binding to backing.

WALL HANGING

Size
36" x 17"

Supplies
Assorted scrap fabrics for appliqués — total of 1/2 yd of 45"w
12 1/2" x 30" piece of light fabric for background
12 1/2" x 14 1/2" piece of medium fabric for small hill
12" x 30" piece of medium fabric for large hill
Light fabric for borders — 1/4 yd of 45"w
Dark fabric for borders — 1/4 yd of 45"w
Binding — 5/8 yd of 45"w fabric
Backing — 5/8 yd of 45"w fabric
Fleece — 5/8 yd of 45"w
Thread to match appliqué fabrics

Cutting Out Pieces
1. Follow **Making Templates**, pg. 147, to make templates from patterns **BB, DD** and **FF-II** on pg. 53. (*Note: Patterns for appliqué templates do not include seam allowances; add seam allowances to these pieces when they are cut out.*)
2. Follow **Cutting Out Quilt Pieces**, pg. 147, and cut out the following:
   BB (roof) — 2 from assorted fabrics
   CC — 2 (3 7/8" x 5") pieces from assorted fabrics
   DD (roof) — 2 from assorted fabrics
   EE — 2 (2 7/8" x 5 3/8") pieces from assorted fabrics
   FF (door) — 2 from assorted fabrics
   GG (window) — 7 from assorted fabrics
   HH (door) — 2 from assorted fabrics
   II (window) — 1 from assorted fabrics
   Road — 1 1/4" x 24" bias strip from assorted fabrics
   Road — 1 1/4" x 12" bias strip from assorted fabrics
   Trees — 1"w bias strips from assorted fabrics
   Border — 3" x 30" piece of light fabric
   Border — 3" x 17" piece of light fabric
   Border — 3" x 30" piece of dark fabric
   Border — 3" x 17" piece of dark fabric
   Binding — 2 (2 1/2" x 17") and 2 (2 1/2" x 36 1/2") pieces

Assembling The Wall Hanging
1. Refer to photo for placement and **Hand Appliqué**, pg. 151, to appliqué small hill to background fabric. Appliqué large hill to background fabric. Trim hill fabrics even with background fabric. Appliqué roads, houses, roofs, doors, and windows to background and hills.

2. For each tree, refer to photo for placement and appliqué bias pieces to background and hills.
3. Sew 30" borders to top and bottom of background. Sew 17" borders to sides of background to complete wall hanging.
4. Follow **Assembling The Quilt**, pg. 155, to layer backing, fleece, and wall hanging and to baste all layers together.
5. Follow **Quilting**, pg. 156, and stitch wall hanging in the ditch along all seamlines and appliqué edges. Trim fleece and backing even with edges of wall hanging.
6. Press one long edge of each binding piece ¹/₄" to wrong side.
7. Matching right sides and raw edges and using a ¹/₄" seam allowance, sew 1 (17") piece to each side of wall hanging. Trim short ends even with wall hanging. Fold binding over to wall hanging backing and pin pressed edge in place covering stitching line. Blind stitch binding to backing.
8. With ends of binding extending ¹/₂" beyond wall hanging on each side, match right sides and raw edges and use a ¹/₄" seam allowance to sew 1 (36¹/₂") piece of binding to top and bottom of wall hanging. Press short ends of binding ¹/₂" to wrong side. Fold binding over to wall hanging backing and pin pressed edge in place covering stitching line. Blind stitch binding to backing.
9. Follow **Making A Hanging Sleeve**, pg. 158, to make and attach hanging sleeve to back of wall hanging.

SCHOOLHOUSE PILLOW

Size
11" x 11"

Supplies
Ecru fabric — ¹/₄ yd of 45"w
Medium blue fabrics (includes backing) — total of ¹/₂ yd of 45"w
Dark blue fabric (includes ruffle) — ¹/₂ yd of 45"w
Muslin for pillow top backing — 15" square
Fleece — 15" square
Polyester fiberfill

Cutting Out Pieces
1. Follow **Making Templates**, pg. 147, to make templates from patterns **A-O** on pgs. 51-53.
2. **Follow Cutting Out Quilt Pieces**, pg. 147, and cut out the following:
   A — 2 from ecru fabric
   B — 1 from medium blue fabric
   B — 1 from dark blue fabric
   C — 1 from ecru fabric
   D — 1 from ecru fabric
   D (reversed) — 1 from ecru fabric
   E — 1 from dark blue fabric
   F — 1 from ecru fabric

G — 1 from medium blue fabric
H — 2 from dark blue fabric
I — 1 from ecru fabric
J — 1 from dark blue fabric
K — 1 from ecru fabric
L — 3 from dark blue fabric
M — 2 from ecru fabric
N — 2 from medium blue fabric
O — 1 from ecru fabric
Sashing — 4 (2" x 9¹/₂") strips from ecru fabric
Setting squares — 4 (2") squares from medium blue fabric

Assembling The Pillow
1. Follow **Steps 1-4** of **Schoolhouse Quilt** to complete 1 **Block**.
2. Follow **Pillow Top** diagram to sew sashing strips and setting squares to **Unit 1** to complete **Pillow Top**.

Pillow Top

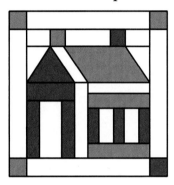

3. Follow **Steps 3-5** of **Making Pillows**, pg. 158, and stitch pillow top in the ditch along all seamlines. Follow **Steps 8-11** to complete pillow.

BROKEN DISHES PILLOW

Size
15" x 13¹/₂"

Supplies
Assorted scrap fabrics (includes backing) — total of ¹/₂ yd of 45"w
Binding (if desired) — ¹/₄ yd of 45"w fabric
Muslin for pillow top backing — 18" square
Fleece — 18" square
Polyester fiberfill

Cutting Out Pieces
1. Follow **Making Templates**, pg. 147, to make templates from patterns **JJ** and **NN** on pg. 53.

2. Follow **Cutting Out Quilt Pieces**, pg. 147, and cut out the following pieces from assorted fabrics:

JJ — 4 pieces
KK — 1 ($2^{1}/_{8}$" x $4^{1}/_{8}$") piece
LL — 1 ($1^{1}/_{2}$" x $4^{1}/_{8}$") piece
MM — 1 (2" x $6^{3}/_{4}$") piece
NN — 8 pieces
OO —1 ($1^{1}/_{4}$" x $6^{3}/_{4}$") piece
PP — 1 (2" x $9^{1}/_{2}$") piece
QQ — 5 ($1^{5}/_{8}$" x $2^{3}/_{8}$") pieces
RR — 1 ($1^{5}/_{8}$" x $9^{1}/_{2}$") piece
SS — 1 (3" x $9^{1}/_{2}$") piece
TT — 1 ($2^{3}/_{4}$" x $10^{1}/_{2}$") piece
UU — 1 ($2^{3}/_{4}$" x 3") piece
VV — 1 (3" x $11^{3}/_{4}$") piece
WW — 1 ($2^{3}/_{4}$" x 3") piece
XX — 1 (2" x $2^{3}/_{4}$") piece
YY — 1 ($2^{3}/_{4}$" x $11^{1}/_{2}$") piece

Assembling The Pillow

1. Follow **Piecing and Pressing**, pg. 148, and **Pillow Top** diagram to sew pieces together in alphabetical order to complete **Pillow Top**.

Pillow Top

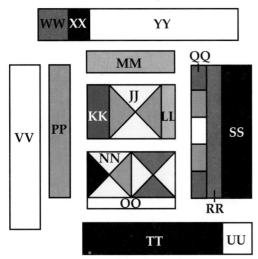

2. Follow **Steps 3-5** of **Making Pillows**, pg. 158, and stitch pillow top in the ditch along all seamlines.
3. If binding is desired, cut a 2" x 66" strip (piece if necessary). With **wrong** sides together, sew pillow backing to pillow top, leaving an opening at bottom edge. Stuff with polyester fiberfill and sew final closure by hand or machine. Matching wrong sides and long edges, fold strip in half; press. Follow **Attaching Binding with Mitered Corners**, pg. 157, to attach binding to pillow.
4. If binding is not desired, follow **Step 11** of **Making Pillows** to finish pillow.

LOG CABIN PILLOW

Size
11" x 11"

Supplies
Assorted fabrics (includes backing) — total of $^{3}/_{4}$ yd of 45"w
Muslin for pillow top backing — 15" square
Ruffle (if desired) — $^{1}/_{3}$ yd of 45"w fabric
Fleece — 15" square
Polyester fiberfill

Cutting Out Pieces

1. Follow **Cutting Out Quilt Pieces**, pg. 147, and cut out the following pieces from assorted fabrics:

ZZ — 1 ($1^{7}/_{8}$" x $2^{1}/_{8}$") piece
AAA — 1 ($1^{3}/_{8}$" x $1^{7}/_{8}$") piece
BBB — 1 ($1^{3}/_{8}$" x 3") piece
CCC —1 ($1^{1}/_{2}$" x $2^{3}/_{4}$") piece
DDD — 1 ($1^{1}/_{2}$" x 4") piece
EEE — 1 ($1^{3}/_{8}$" x $3^{3}/_{4}$") piece
FFF — 1 ($1^{3}/_{8}$" x $4^{7}/_{8}$") piece
GGG — 1 ($1^{1}/_{4}$" x $4^{5}/_{8}$") piece
HHH — 1 ($1^{1}/_{4}$" x $5^{5}/_{8}$") piece
III — 1 ($1^{1}/_{2}$" x $5^{3}/_{8}$") piece
JJJ — 1 ($1^{1}/_{2}$" x $6^{5}/_{8}$") piece
KKK — 1 ($1^{3}/_{4}$" x $6^{3}/_{8}$") piece
LLL — 1 ($1^{3}/_{4}$" x $7^{7}/_{8}$") piece
MMM — 1 ($1^{3}/_{4}$" x $7^{5}/_{8}$") piece
NNN — 1 ($1^{3}/_{4}$" x $9^{1}/_{8}$") piece
OOO — 2 ($1^{3}/_{8}$" x $2^{5}/_{8}$") pieces
PPP — 1 ($1^{3}/_{8}$" x $6^{3}/_{4}$") piece
QQQ — 1 ($1^{3}/_{8}$" x $7^{7}/_{8}$") piece
RRR — 1 (1" x $9^{3}/_{4}$") piece
SSS — 1 ($1^{1}/_{8}$" x $10^{1}/_{2}$") piece
TTT — 1 ($1^{1}/_{2}$" x $10^{3}/_{8}$") piece
UUU — 1 ($1^{7}/_{8}$" x $11^{1}/_{2}$") piece

Assembling The Pillow

1. Follow **Piecing and Pressing**, pg. 148, and **Pillow Top Diagram** and sew pieces together in alphabetical order to complete **Pillow Top**.

Pillow Top

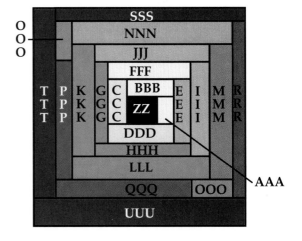

2. Follow **Steps 3-5** of **Making Pillows**, pg. 158, and stitch pillow top in the ditch along seamlines. If ruffle is desired, follow **Steps 8-11** to complete pillow. If ruffle is not desired, follow **Step 11** to complete pillow.

HOLE IN THE BARN DOOR PILLOW

Size

15¹/₂″ x 13″

Supplies

Assorted light fabrics (includes backing) — total of ¹/₂ yd of 45″w
Assorted medium fabrics — total of ¹/₂ yd of 45″w
Assorted dark fabrics — total of ¹/₄ yd of 45″w
Binding — ¹/₄ yd of 45″w fabric
Muslin for pillow top backing — 22″ x 20″ piece
Fleece — 22″ x 20″ piece
Polyester fiberfill

Cutting Out Pieces

1. Follow **Making Templates**, pg. 147, to make template from pattern **Q** on pg. 52.
2. Follow **Cutting Out Quilt Pieces**, pg. 147, and cut out the following:
   Q — 4 from light fabrics
   Q — 4 from dark fabrics
   R — 4 (1⁷/₈″ x 3″) pieces from light fabrics
   S — 1 (3″) square from medium fabrics
   T — 4 (1⁷/₈″ x 5³/₄″) pieces from dark fabrics
   U — 4 (1⁷/₈″) squares from dark fabrics
   V — 1 (1″ x 8¹/₂″) piece from medium fabrics
   W — 1 (1¹/₄″ x 9″) piece from medium fabrics
   X — 1 (1¹/₈″ x 9″) piece from light fabrics
   Setting blocks — 4 (2¹/₄″ x 4″) pieces from dark fabrics
   Sashing — 2 (4″ x 9⁷/₈″) strips from medium fabrics
   Sashing — 2 (2¹/₄″ x 9¹/₂″) strips from medium fabrics
   Binding — 2″ x 65″ piece (piece if necessary)

Assembling The Pillow

1. Follow **Step 1** of **Hole In The Barn Door Table Rug** to make 1 **Unit 2**.
2. Follow **Pillow Top** diagram to sew remaining pieces, sashing strips, and setting blocks to **Unit 2** to complete **Pillow Top**.

Pillow Top

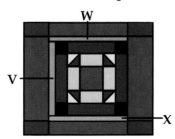

3. Follow **Steps 3-5** of **Making Pillows**, pg. 158, and stitch pillow top in the ditch along seamlines.
4. With wrong sides together, sew pillow backing to pillow top, leaving an opening at bottom edge. Stuff with polyester fiberfill and sew final closure by hand or machine.
5. Matching wrong sides and long edges, fold binding piece in half; press. Follow **Attaching Binding with Mitered Corners**, pg. 157, to attach binding to pillow.

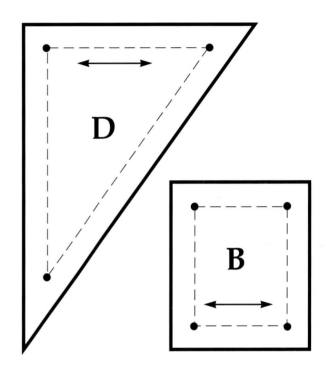

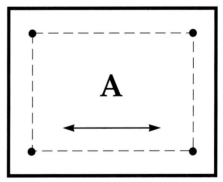

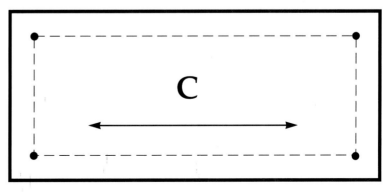

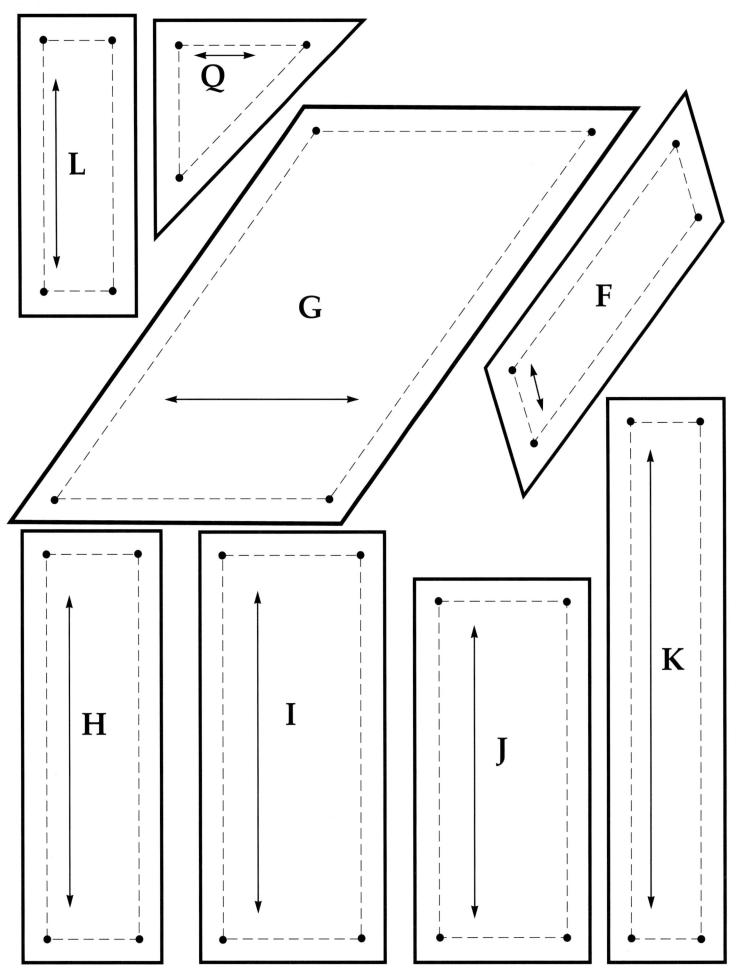

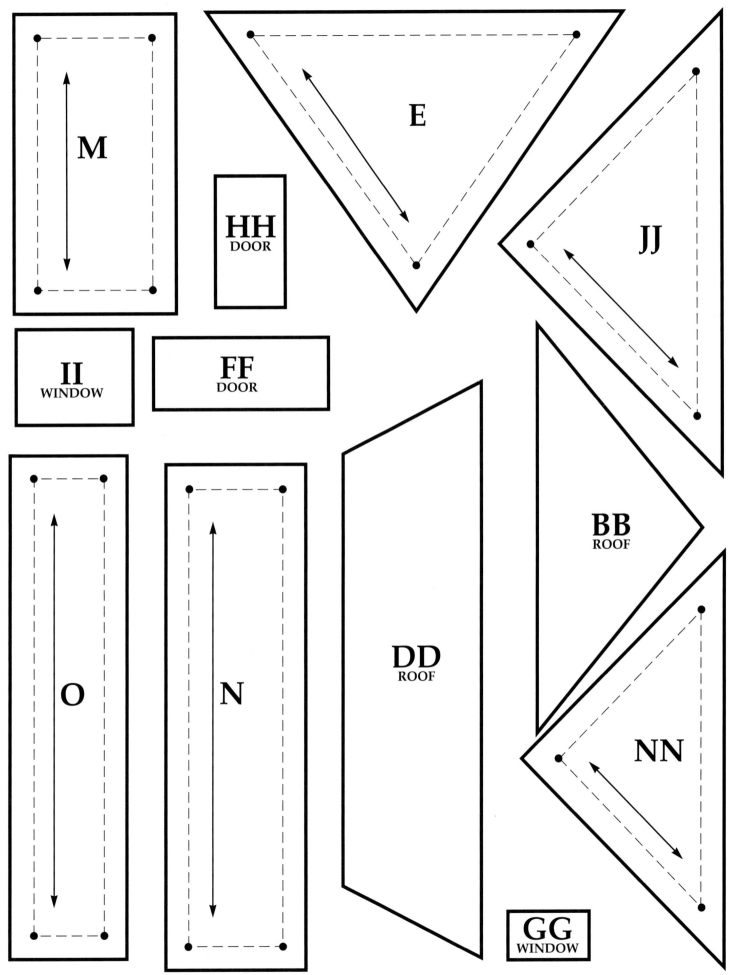

BABY QUILTS

The arrival of a new baby is always a joyous occasion, awaited with eager anticipation. Long before the expected birth date, the nursery is prepared with carefully chosen furniture, wallpaper, and toys. Adding to the excitement, friends and family shower mother and baby with gifts. Handmade baby quilts are among the most special of these offerings. Stitched with love, each one is a tiny treasure that is sure to become a cherished heirloom for future generations. The dainty pink and white Dresden Plate quilt pictured here is perfect for a little girl. Quilted hearts and a Prairie Point edging provide a delicate finish.

This variation of the popular old Bow Tie pattern makes a handsome quilt for a baby boy. Blocks of ticking-striped fabric and a Prairie Point edging add extra appeal.

DRESDEN PLATE

Size
Block: 12″ x 12″
Quilt: 49″ x 64″

Yardage Requirements
White fabric for background blocks and setting
  squares — 1½ yds of 45″w
Pink fabric for blocks and sashing — 2 yds of 45″w
Pink print fabric — ¾ yd of 45″w
White fabric for prairie points — ⅞ yd of 45″w
Backing — 3¾ yds of 45″w **OR** 1⅞ yds of 90″w
72″ x 90″ piece of low-loft polyester bonded
  batting

Cutting Out Pieces
1. Follow **Making Templates**, pg. 147, to make
   templates from patterns **A** and **B** on pg. 59.
   (*Note: Pattern for appliqué template **B** does not
   include seam allowance; add seam allowance when
   pieces are cut out.*)
2. To complete our quilt you will need 12 blocks.
   Follow **Cutting Out Quilt Pieces**, pg. 147, and
   cut out the following:
   Sashing — 31 (3″ x 12½″) pieces from pink
     fabric
   Setting squares — 20 (3″) squares from white
     fabric
   Prairie Points — 116 (3″) squares from white
     fabric
   A — 96 from pink fabric
   A — 96 from pink print fabric
   B — 12 from pink fabric
   C — 12 (12½″) squares from white fabric

Assembling The Quilt
1. For each block, follow **Piecing And Pressing**,
   pg. 148, to sew 8 pink **A's** to 8 pink print **A's** to
   make **Unit 1**. (*Note: If machine piecing, sew only to
   the dots when joining these pieces; the seam
   allowances above the dots must be left free in order to
   turn under for appliqué.*) Press outer raw edges
   ¼″ to wrong side.

Unit 1

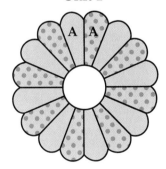

2. Follow **Hand Appliqué**, pg. 151, to appliqué 1 **B**
   to center of **Unit 1**.
3. Fold 1 **C** in half from top to bottom; finger press
   and unfold. Fold in half from left to right; finger
   press and unfold. Using fold lines as a guide,
   center and baste **Unit 1** to **C**. Appliqué **Unit 1** to **C**
   to complete **Block**.

Block

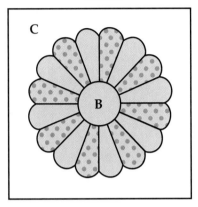

4. Repeat to make 12 **Blocks**.
5. Sew 3 **Blocks** between 4 sashing strips to make
   Row 1. Repeat to make **Rows 2-4**.

Row 1

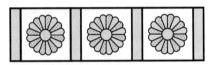

6. Sew 3 sashing strips between 4 setting squares to
   make **Unit 2**. Repeat to make a total of 5 **Unit 2's**.

Unit 2

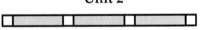

7. Sew **Row 1** between 2 **Unit 2's**. Repeat to add
   Rows 2-4 and remaining **Unit 2's** to complete
   Quilt Top.

Quilt Top

8. For prairie points, fold 1 square in half diagonally, forming a triangle *(Fig. 1)*; press. Matching folded edges, fold in half again *(Fig. 2)*; press. Repeat with remaining fabric squares.

Fig. 1   **Fig. 2**

9. Beginning at upper left corner of quilt top and matching raw edges, pin first prairie point to quilt top with closed side of prairie point facing left. Add second prairie point by slipping closed side approximately 3/4" inside open side of first prairie point *(Fig. 3)*. *(Note: After pinning prairie points to each side of quilt, it may be necessary to readjust slightly by overlapping more or less to fit edge of quilt top.)* Pin 25 prairie points to each short edge and 33 prairie points to each long edge of quilt top. Sew prairie points to quilt top using a 1/4" seam allowance.

Fig. 3

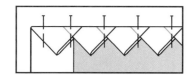

10. Press prairie points out, pressing seam allowances toward quilt top.
11. Follow **Marking Quilting Lines**, pg. 154, and **Quilting Diagram** and **Quilting Patterns**, pg. 59, to mark quilting lines on quilt top.

Quilting Diagram

12. Follow **Preparing Backing And Batting**, pg. 155, to piece backing if necessary.
13. Follow **Assembling The Quilt**, pg. 155, to layer backing, batting, and quilt top and to baste all layers together.
14. Follow **Quilting**, pg. 156, and stitch quilt along marked lines.

15. Trim batting even with seamline of prairie points. Trim backing 1/4" larger than batting. Press raw edges of backing 1/4" to wrong side. Pin pressed edge in place covering stitching line. Blind stitch backing to quilt.

BOW TIE

Size
Block: 12" x 12"
Quilt: 49" x 64"

Yardage Requirements
White fabric for blocks and setting squares —
  3/4 yd of 45"w
Light blue fabric for sashing — 1 1/8 yds of 45"w
Blue print fabric — 1/2 yd of 45"w
Blue stripe fabric — 7/8 yd of 45"w
Dark blue fabric — 1/4 yd of 45"w
White fabric for prairie points —7/8 yd of 45"w
Backing — 3 3/4 yds of 45"w **OR** 1 7/8 yds of 90"w
72" x 90" piece of low-loft polyester bonded batting

Cutting Out Pieces
1. Follow **Making Templates**, pg. 147, to make templates from patterns **D** and **E** on pg. 59.
2. To complete our quilt you will need 12 blocks. Follow **Cutting Out Quilt Pieces**, pg. 147, to cut out the following:
   Sashing — 31 (3" x 12 1/2") pieces from light blue fabric
   Setting squares — 20 (3") squares from white fabric
   Prairie Points — 116 (3") squares from white fabric
   D — 48 from blue print fabric
   D — 48 from white fabric
   E — 24 from dark blue fabric
   F — 24 (6 1/2") squares from blue stripe fabric

Assembling The Quilt
1. For each block, follow **Piecing And Pressing**, pg. 148, to sew 2 blue print **D's** to 1 **E** to make **Unit 1**. *(Note: If machine piecing, sew only between the dots when joining these pieces; the seam allowances must be left free in order to set in seams.)* Repeat to make a total of 2 **Unit 1's**. Follow **Sewing Into A Corner**, pg. 150, and sew 2 white **D's** to 1 **Unit 1** to make **Unit 2**. Repeat to make a total of 2 **Unit 2's**.

Unit 1   Unit 2

2. Sew 2 **F's** to 2 **Unit 2's** to complete **Block**.

Block

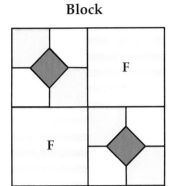

3. Repeat to make 12 **Blocks**.
4. Follow **Steps 5-7** of **Dresden Plate** to complete **Quilt Top**.

Quilt Top

5. Follow **Steps 8-15** of **Dresden Plate** to complete quilt using **Quilting Diagram** and **Quilting Pattern** for **Bow Tie** quilt.

Quilting Diagram

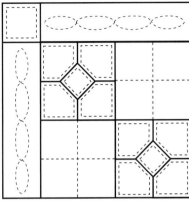

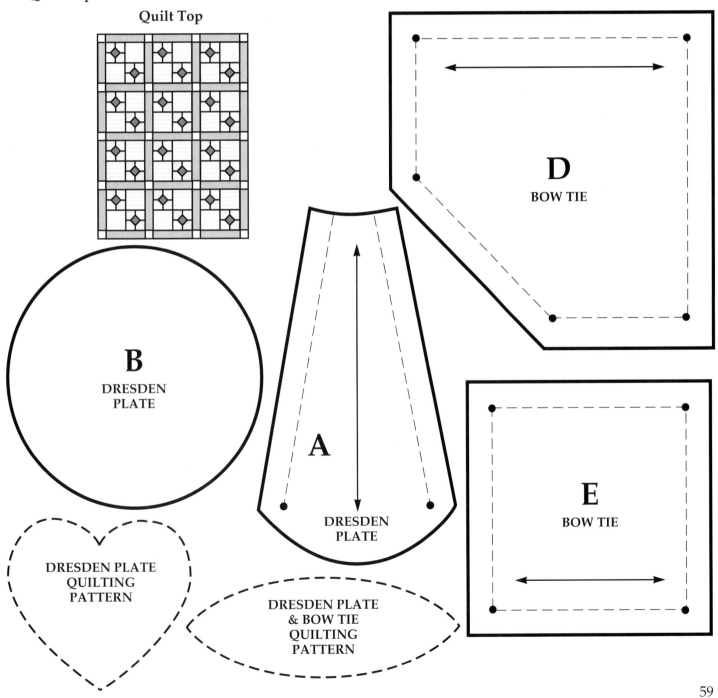

B
DRESDEN
PLATE

A
DRESDEN
PLATE

D
BOW TIE

E
BOW TIE

DRESDEN PLATE
QUILTING
PATTERN

DRESDEN PLATE
& BOW TIE
QUILTING
PATTERN

CHURN DASH COLLECTION

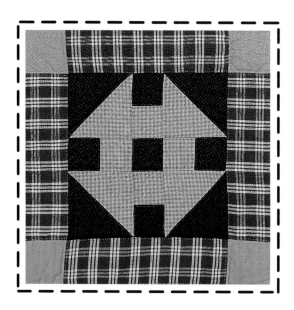

The names of many enduring quilt patterns reflect aspects of household chores in years gone by. Churning fresh milk into sweet, creamy butter was a common task for most housewives until the latter part of the 1800's, when creameries began to produce large quantities of butter. The classic Churn Dash pattern, with its simple geometric shapes, is reminiscent of those old-time churns. Bringing to mind images of hearth and home, the colorful quilt here is pieced in all-American red, white, and blue fabrics with touches of black and tan. To complement the traditional design, we created the kitchen accessories shown on the following pages.

Homespun plaids add warmth to this country collection. Table runners placed horizontally can double as place mats. As useful as they are attractive, these potholders are pieced in three color schemes. Shown on page 64, a quilt block bib adds charm to our simple apron.

CHURN DASH QUILT

Size
Block: 8³/₄" x 8³/₄"
Quilt: 72" x 81"

Yardage Requirements
Assorted light fabrics — total of 2 yds of 45"w
Assorted dark fabrics — total of 2 yds of 45"w
Red fabric for sashing — 2¹/₄ yds of 45"w
Tan fabric for setting squares — ³/₄ yd of 45"w
Blue fabric for borders — ¹/₄ yd of 45"w
Binding — ¹/₂ yd of 45"w fabric
Backing — 5 yds of 45"w fabric **OR** 2¹/₂ yds of 90"w fabric
81" x 96" piece of low-loft polyester bonded batting

Cutting Out Pieces
1. Follow **Making Templates**, pg. 147, to make templates from patterns **A** and **B** on pg. 69.
2. To complete our quilt you will need 30 blocks. Follow **Cutting Out Quilt Pieces**, pg. 147, and cut out the following:
   Sashing — 71 (4¹/₂" x 9¹/₄") pieces from red fabric
   Setting squares — 42 (4¹/₂") squares from tan fabric
   Borders — 2 (2¹/₄" x 79¹/₂") pieces from blue fabric
   Binding — 2 (1¹/₂" x 72") pieces
   Binding — 2 (1¹/₂" x 81") pieces
   A — 120 from assorted light fabrics
   A — 120 from assorted dark fabrics
   B — 150 from assorted light fabrics
   B — 120 from assorted dark fabrics

Assembling The Quilt
1. For each block, follow **Piecing And Pressing**, pg. 148, and **Unit 1** diagram to sew pieces together to make **Unit 1**. Repeat to make a total of 2 **Unit 1's**.

Unit 1

2. Follow **Unit 2** diagram and sew pieces together to make **Unit 2**.

Unit 2

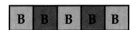

3. Follow **Block** diagram and sew **Unit 2** between 2 **Unit 1's** to complete **Block**.

Block

4. Repeat to make 30 **Blocks**.
5. Sew 5 **Blocks** between 6 sashing strips to make **Row 1**. Repeat to make **Rows 2-6**.

Row 1

6. Sew 5 sashing strips between 6 setting squares to make **Unit 3**. Repeat to make a total of 7 **Unit 3's**.

Unit 3

7. Sew **Row 1** between 2 **Unit 3's**. Repeat to add **Rows 2-6** and remaining **Unit 3's** to make **Unit 4**.

Unit 4

8. Sew 1 border to each side of **Unit 4** to complete **Quilt Top**.

Quilt Top

9. Our antique quilt was quilted in randomly placed radiating circles approximately 1¼" apart beginning in the corners of the quilt and meeting in the center. Follow **Marking Quilting Lines**, pg. 154, and refer to photo and **Quilting Diagram** to mark quilting lines on quilt top.

Quilting Diagram

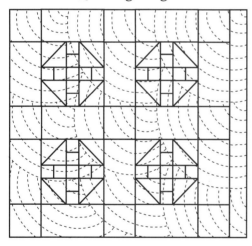

10. Follow **Preparing Backing And Batting**, pg. 155, to piece backing if necessary.
11. Follow **Assembling The Quilt**, pg. 155, to layer backing, batting, and quilt top and to baste all layers together.
12. Follow **Quilting**, pg. 156, and stitch quilt along marked lines. Trim batting and backing even with edges of quilt.
13. Press one long edge of each binding piece ¼" to wrong side. Matching right sides and raw edges and using a ¼" seam allowance, sew 1 (72") piece of binding each to top and bottom of quilt. Trim short ends even with quilt. Fold binding over to quilt backing and pin pressed edge in place, covering stitching line. Blind stitch binding to backing.

14. With ends of binding extending ½" beyond quilt on each side, match right sides and raw edges and use a ¼" seam allowance to sew 1 (81") piece of binding to each side of quilt. Press short ends of binding ½" to wrong side. Fold binding over to quilt backing and pin pressed edge in place, covering stitching line. Blind stitch binding to backing.

CHURN DASH APRON

Size
Block: 8¾" x 8¾"
Apron: 34½" x 33" (not including ties)

Yardage Requirements
Light fabric — 10" square
Dark fabric — 10" square
Backing — 12" square
12" square of fleece
Red fabric for block binding, apron skirt, and neck ties — 1¼ yds of 45"w
Black fabric for apron waistband and ties — ⅜ yd of 45"w fabric

Cutting Out Pieces
1. Follow **Making Templates**, pg. 147, to make templates from patterns **A** and **B** on pg. 69.
2. Follow **Cutting Out Quilt Pieces**, pg. 147, and cut out the following:
   A — 4 from light fabric
   A — 4 from dark fabric
   B — 4 from light fabric
   B — 5 from dark fabric
   Block binding — 1 (2½" x 30") bias strip from red fabric
   Apron skirt — 1 (35" x 25½") piece from red fabric
   Neck Ties — 2 (2" x 28") bias strips from red fabric
   Waistband — 1 (5" x 70") piece (pieced if necessary)

Making The Apron
1. Follow **Steps 1-3** of **Churn Dash Quilt** to complete 1 block.
2. Follow **Marking Quilting Lines**, pg. 154, and **Quilting Diagram** to mark quilting lines on block.

Quilting Diagram

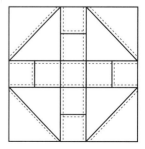

3. Follow **Assembling The Quilt**, pg. 155, to layer backing, fleece, and block and to baste all layers together.
4. Follow **Quilting**, pg. 156, and stitch block along marked lines. Trim fleece and backing even with block.
5. Follow **Attaching Binding With Mitered Corners**, pg. 157, and use the 30" bias strip to bind three sides of block.
6. Press each short edge and one long edge of skirt 1/2" to wrong side; press 1/2" to wrong side again and stitch in place. Baste 1/2" and 1/4" from raw edge. Pull basting threads, drawing up gathers to measure 13 1/2".
7. *Note: Use 1/2" seam allowance for all seams.* Press each short edge and one long edge of waistband 1/2" to wrong side. Matching right sides, raw edges, and centers, baste gathered edge of skirt to waistband. Press seam toward waistband pressing remaining raw edges of waistband 1/2" to wrong side. Matching wrong sides and long edges fold waistband in half; press. Topstitch close to folded edges.
8. Matching centers, lap top of waistband 1/4" over unfinished edge of block; topstitch in place.
9. For neck ties, press short edges of each bias strip 1/2" to wrong side. Matching wrong sides and long edges, fold each strip in half and press. Fold raw edges of each strip to center and press. Topstitch close to folded edges of each strip. Hand sew ties to upper corners on wrong side of block.

TABLE RUNNER

Size
Block: 8 3/4" x 8 3/4"
Table Runner: 63" x 18"

Yardage Requirements
Assorted fabrics — total of 3/4 yd of 45"w
Red plaid fabric for sashing — 5/8 yd of 45"w
Tan fabric for setting squares— 1/8 yd of 45"w
Blue fabric for border— 3/8 yd of 45"w
Red fabric for border — 1/4 yd of 45"w
Binding — 3/4 yd of 45"w fabric
Backing — 1 1/8 yds of 45"w fabric
70" x 24" piece of fleece

Cutting Out Pieces
1. Follow **Making Templates**, pg. 147, to make templates from patterns **A** and **B** on pg. 69.
2. To complete 1 table runner you will need 5 blocks. Follow **Cutting Out Quilt Pieces**, pg. 147, and cut out the following:
   A — 40 from assorted fabrics
   B — 45 from assorted fabrics
   Sashing — 16 (3" x 9 1/4") pieces from red plaid fabric
   Setting squares — 12 (3") squares from tan fabric
   Blue border — 2 (1 1/4" x 59 1/4") and 2 (1 1/4" x 15 3/4") pieces from blue fabric
   Red border — 2 (1 1/2" x 60 3/4") and 2 (1 1/2" x 17 3/4") pieces from red fabric

Assembling The Table Runner
1. Follow **Steps 1-3** of **Churn Dash Quilt** to make 5 blocks.
2. Sew 5 blocks between 6 sashing strips to make **Unit 1**.

Unit 1

3. Sew 5 sashing strips between 6 setting squares to make **Unit 2**. Repeat to make a total of 2 **Unit 2's**.

Unit 2

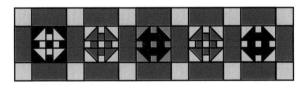

4. Sew **Unit 1** between **Unit 2's** to make **Unit 3**.

Unit 3

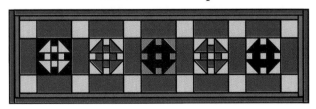

5. Follow **Table Runner Top** diagram and sew borders to **Unit 3** to make **Table Runner Top**.

Table Runner Top

6. Follow **Marking Quilting Lines**, pg. 154, and **Quilting Diagram** to mark quilting lines on table runner top.

Quilting Diagram

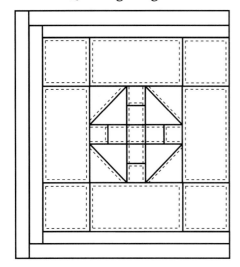

7. Follow **Preparing Backing And Batting**, pg. 155, to piece backing.
8. Follow **Assembling The Quilt**, pg. 155, to layer backing, fleece, and table runner top and to baste all layers together.
9. Follow **Quilting**, pg. 156, and stitch table runner along marked lines. Trim fleece and backing even with edges of table runner.
10. Follow **Making Continuous Bias Strip Binding**, pg. 156, and use a 27" square to make 5 yds of 2¹/₂"w bias binding.
11. Follow **Attaching Binding With Mitered Corners**, pg. 157, and attach bias binding to table runner.

POTHOLDER

Size
7¹/₂" x 7¹/₂"

Yardage Requirements
Light fabric — 10" square
Dark fabric — 10" square
Binding — ¹/₄ yd of 45"w fabric
Backing — 10" square
10" square of fleece

Cutting Out Pieces
1. Follow **Making Templates**, pg. 147, to make templates from patterns **C** and **D** on pg. 69.
2. To complete each potholder you will need 1 block. Follow **Cutting Out Quilt Pieces**, pg. 147, and cut out the following:
   C — 4 from light fabric
   C — 4 from dark fabric
   D — 5 from light fabric
   D — 4 from dark fabric

Assembling The Potholder
1. Follow **Steps 1-3** of **Churn Dash Quilt** substituting patterns **C** and **D** for **A** and **B** to make 1 block.
2. Follow **Marking Quilting Lines**, pg. 154, and **Quilting Diagram** to mark quilting lines on block.

Quilting Diagram

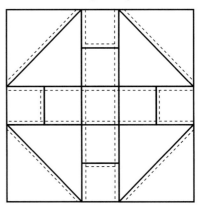

3. Follow **Assembling The Quilt**, pg. 155, to layer backing, fleece, and block and to baste all layers together.
4. Follow **Quilting**, pg. 156, and stitch block along marked lines. Trim fleece and backing even with edges of block.
5. For binding, cut a 2¹/₂" x 32" bias strip (pieced if necessary). Matching wrong sides and long edges, fold strip in half; press.
6. Follow **Attaching Binding With Mitered Corners**, pg. 157, and attach bias binding to block to complete potholder.

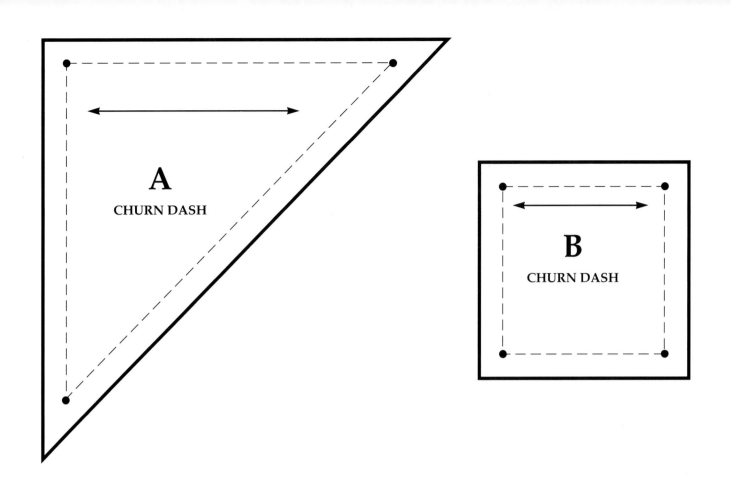

A

CHURN DASH

B

CHURN DASH

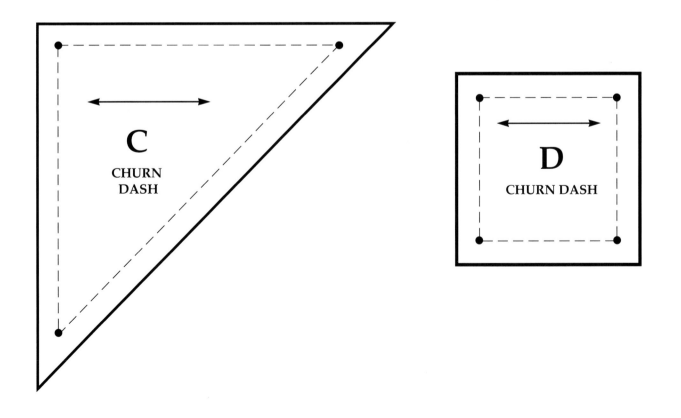

C

CHURN
DASH

D

CHURN DASH

QUILT BLOCK SAMPLER

In years past, quilters often pieced ''sampler'' quilts containing
a variety of their favorite patterns. Sometimes the blocks were included
because the quilter liked the designs; often they were a part of a pattern
collection that the seamstress used for reference. Created on a smaller scale,
our sampler wall hanging includes a number of popular designs, many
of which have been shown in other settings in this volume. One
of the blocks contains the quiltmaker's embroidered signature,
adding interest for future generations. A carefully chosen
color scheme unifies the attractive piece.

QUILT BLOCK SAMPLER WALL HANGING

Size
32" x 42"

Yardage Requirements
Assorted tan fabrics — total of 1 yd of 45"w
Assorted teal fabrics — total of 1 yd of 45"w
Assorted purple fabrics — total of 1 yd of 45"w
Assorted black fabrics — total of 1/2 yd of 45"w
Tan fabric for borders — 1 1/8 yds of 45"w
Teal fabric for borders — 1 1/8 yds of 45"w
Binding — 3/4 yd of 45"w teal fabric
Backing — 1 yd of 45"w fabric
Fleece — 1 yd of 45"w
Six strand embroidery floss
Metallic thread
Glass seed beads and 3mm pearls

Block A
1. Follow **Making Templates**, pg. 147, to make templates from patterns **A** and **B** on pg. 69.
2. Follow **Cutting Out Quilt Pieces**, pg. 147, and cut out the following:
   A — 4 from tan fabric
   A — 4 from teal fabric
   B — 4 from tan fabric
   B — 5 from purple fabric
3. Follow **Assembling The Quilt, Steps 1-3** of **Churn Dash Quilt**, pg. 65, to complete **Block A**.

Block B
1. Cut out the following:
   A — 4 (2 1/2") squares from tan fabric
   A — 2 (2 1/2") squares from teal fabric
   A — 2 (2 1/2") squares from purple fabric
2. Follow **Piecing and Pressing**, pg. 148, and **Block B** diagram to sew pieces together to complete **Block B**.

Block B

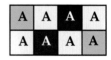

Block C
1. Make templates from patterns **A-G** on pgs. 76-77. Cut out the following:
   A — 1 from tan fabric
   B — 1 from tan fabric
   C — 1 from teal fabric
   D —1 from purple fabric
   E — 1 from purple fabric
   F — 1 from teal fabric
   G — 1 from teal fabric
2. Follow **Block C** diagram and sew pieces together in alphabetical order to complete **Block C**.

Block C

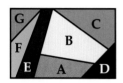

Block D
1. Make template from pattern **R** on pg. 97. Cut out the following:
   R — 16 from purple fabric
   R — 16 from tan fabric
   S — 4 (1 1/2") squares from tan fabric
   S — 1 (1 1/2") square from purple fabric
   T — 4 (2 1/2") squares from teal fabric
   U — 4 (1 1/2" x 3 1/2") pieces from tan fabric
2. Follow **Assembling The Quilt, Steps 1-5** of **Bear's Paw Quilt**, pg. 90, substituting **R-U** for **A-D** to complete **Block D**.

Block E
1. Make template from pattern **K** on pg. 78. Cut out the following:
   H — 2 (1 1/4" x 2 1/2") pieces from teal fabric
   I — 1 (2" x 2 1/2") piece from purple fabric
   J — 1 (2 1/2" x 3") piece from teal fabric
   K — 4 from tan fabric
   K — 4 from teal fabric
   L — 1 (1 3/4" x 5 1/2") piece from tan fabric
   M — 1 (1 1/4" x 5 1/2") piece from teal fabric
2. Sew **I** and **J** between **H's** to make **Unit 1**.

Unit 1

3. Follow **Unit 2** diagram and sew pieces together to make **Unit 2**.

Unit 2

4. Sew **L** to **M** to make **Unit 3**.

Unit 3

5. Sew **Unit 1**, **Unit 2**, and **Unit 3** together to complete **Block E**.

Block E

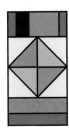

Block F

1. Make templates from patterns **A-O** on pgs. 51-53. Cut out the following:
   A — 2 from tan fabric
   B — 2 from black fabric
   C — 1 from tan fabric
   D — 1 from tan fabric
   D (reversed) — 1 from tan fabric
   E — 1 from purple fabric
   F — 1 from black fabric
   G — 1 from purple fabric
   H — 2 from teal fabric
   I — 1 from purple fabric
   J — 1 from teal fabric
   K — 1 from black fabric
   L — 3 from teal fabric
   M — 2 from purple fabric
   N — 2 from teal fabric
   O — 1 from black fabric
2. Follow **Assembling The Quilt, Steps 1-4** of **Schoolhouse Quilt**, pg. 46, to complete **Block F**.

Block G

1. Make template from pattern **N** on pg. 78. Cut out the following:
   N — 12 from tan fabric
   N — 12 from teal fabric
2. Follow **Block G** diagram to sew **N**'s together to complete **Block G**.

Block G

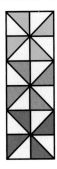

Block H

1. Make templates from patterns **O-Q** on pg. 78. Cut out the following:
   O — 2 from purple fabric
   P — 2 from teal fabric
   Q — 8 from teal fabric
   Q — 8 from purple fabric
2. Follow **Unit 1** diagram to sew pieces together to make **Unit 1**.

Unit 1

3. Follow **Unit 2** diagram to sew **Q**'s together to make **Unit 2**.

Unit 2

4. Sew **Unit 1** to **Unit 2** to complete **Block H**.

Block H

Block I

1. Make templates from patterns **R** and **T-Y** on pgs. 78-79. Cut out the following:
   R — 9 from purple fabric
   R — 6 from teal fabric
   S — 2 ($1^{1}/_{2}$" x $3^{1}/_{2}$") pieces from teal fabric
   T — 1 from purple fabric
   U — 1 from teal fabric
   V — 1 from purple fabric
   W — 1 from teal fabric
   X — 4 from purple fabric
   Y — 4 from tan fabric
2. Follow **Assembling The Quilt, Steps 1-7** of **Basket Quilt**, pg. 27, to complete 1 block, substituting patterns **R-W** for **A-F**.
3. Sew 1 **X** and 1 **Y** to each corner to complete **Block I**.

Block I

Block J

1. Cut out the following:
   Z — 1 ($1^{7}/_{8}$" x $2^{1}/_{8}$") piece from purple fabric
   AA — 1 ($1^{3}/_{8}$" x $1^{7}/_{8}$") piece from purple fabric
   BB — 1 ($1^{3}/_{8}$" x 3") piece from purple fabric
   CC — 1 ($1^{1}/_{2}$" x $2^{3}/_{4}$") piece from teal fabric
   DD — 1 ($1^{1}/_{2}$" x 4") piece from teal fabric
   EE — 1 ($1^{3}/_{8}$" x $3^{3}/_{4}$") piece from purple fabric
   FF — 1 ($1^{3}/_{8}$" x $4^{7}/_{8}$") piece from purple fabric
   GG — 1 ($1^{1}/_{4}$" x $4^{5}/_{8}$") piece from teal fabric
   HH — 1 ($1^{1}/_{4}$" x $5^{5}/_{8}$") piece from teal fabric
   II — 1 ($1^{1}/_{2}$" x $5^{3}/_{8}$") piece from purple fabric
   JJ — 1 ($1^{1}/_{2}$" x $6^{5}/_{8}$") piece from purple fabric
   KK — 1 ($1^{3}/_{4}$" x $6^{3}/_{8}$") piece from teal fabric
   LL — 1 ($1^{3}/_{4}$" x $7^{7}/_{8}$") piece from teal fabric
   MM — 1 ($1^{3}/_{4}$" x $7^{5}/_{8}$") piece from purple fabric
   NN — 1 ($1^{3}/_{4}$" x $9^{1}/_{8}$") piece from purple fabric
   OO — 1 ($1^{3}/_{8}$" x $8^{7}/_{8}$") piece from black fabric
   PP — 1 ($1^{3}/_{8}$" x 10") piece from black fabric
   QQ — 2 ($2^{1}/_{2}$") squares from black fabric
   QQ — 3 ($2^{1}/_{2}$") squares from teal fabric
   QQ — 4 ($2^{1}/_{2}$") squares from purple fabric
   RR — 1 ($8^{1}/_{2}$") square from tan fabric
   Binding — $^{3}/_{4}$" x 24" bias strip from purple fabric

2. Follow **Log Cabin Block** diagram to sew **Z-PP** together in alphabetical order to make 1 **Log Cabin Block**.

Log Cabin Block

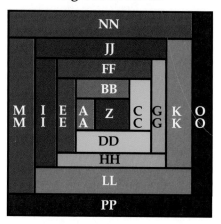

3. Use heart pattern, pg. 79, to cut heart shape from **Log Cabin Block**. Matching right sides and raw edges, sew binding to heart using a $^{1}/_{8}$" seam allowance. Fold binding over to wrong side of heart and press.
4. Follow **Block J** diagram to sew **QQ's** to **RR**. Follow **Hand Appliqué**, pg. 151, to appliqué heart to **RR** to complete **Block J**.

Block J

Block K

1. Cut out the following:
   U — 10 from tan fabric
   U — 10 from teal fabric
2. Follow **Block K** diagram and sew **U's** together to complete **Block K**.

Block K

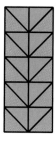

Block L

1. Make templates from patterns **A** and **B** on pg. 59. Cut out the following:
   A — 6 from purple fabric
   A — 6 from teal fabric
   A — 4 from black fabric
   B — 1 from tan fabric
   C — 1 (10½″) square from tan fabric
2. Follow **Assembling The Quilt, Steps 1-3** of **Dresden Plate Quilt**, pg. 57, to complete **Block L**.

Block M

1. Use template **U** from **Block I** and cut out the following:
   U — 8 from tan fabric
   U — 8 from teal fabric
   SS — 1 (1¼″ x 8½″) piece from tan fabric
   TT — 1 (1¾″ x 8½″) piece from teal fabric
2. Follow **Block M** diagram to sew pieces together to complete **Block M**.

Block M

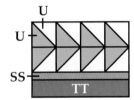

Block N

1. Use template **U** from **Block I** and cut out the following:
   U — 4 from black fabric
   U — 4 from purple fabric
   UU — 4 (2½″) squares from teal fabric
   VV — 2 (2½″ x 4½″) pieces from tan fabric
   WW — 1 (2½″ x 6″) piece from tan fabric
2. Follow **Unit 1** diagram and sew pieces together to make **Unit 1**. Repeat to make a total of 2 **Unit 1's.**

Unit 1

3. Follow **Block N** diagram to sew pieces together to complete **Block N**.

Block N

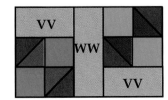

Block O

1. Use template **Q** from **Block H** and cut out the following:
   Q — 4 from tan fabric
   Q — 12 from purple fabric
   XX — 4 (2½″) squares from tan fabric
   XX — 1 (2½″) square from purple fabric
2. Follow **Unit 1** diagram to sew pieces together to make **Unit 1**. Repeat to make a total of 2 **Unit 1's.**

Unit 1

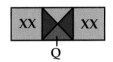

3. Follow **Unit 2** diagram to make **Unit 2**.

Unit 2

4. Follow **Block O** diagram to sew **Unit 1's** and **Unit 2** together to complete **Block O**.

Block O

Assembling The Wall Hanging

1. Follow **Assembly Diagram** to sew blocks **A-O** together to make **Wall Hanging Top**.

Assembly Diagram

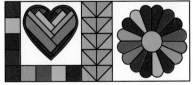

2. To embellish **Block C**, use 3 strands of embroidery floss or 1 strand of metallic thread as desired for all embroidery stitches. Refer to **Stitch Diagrams**, pg. 159, to embroider block as desired. Add seed beads or 3mm pearls as desired. Lightly sign name with #2 pencil in center of block; **Outline Stitch** name.

3. Cut out the following:
   YY — 4 (2¹/₂″) squares from black fabric
   YY — 8 (2¹/₂″) squares from teal fabric
   YY — 4 (2¹/₂″) squares from purple fabric
   Border — 2 (2¹/₂″ x 24³/₄″) pieces from tan fabric
   Border — 2 (2¹/₂″ x 24³/₄″) pieces from teal fabric
   Border — 2 (2¹/₂″ x 35″) pieces from tan fabric
   Border — 2 (2¹/₂″ x 35″) pieces from teal fabric

4. Follow **Wall Hanging Top** diagram to sew 4 **YY's** together to make each corner block.

5. Sew 1 (24³/₄″) tan piece to 1 (24³/₄″) teal piece to make top border. Repeat to make bottom border. Sew 1 (35″) tan piece to 1 (35″) teal piece to make side border. Repeat to make 2 side borders. Sew 1 corner block to each end of each side border.

6. Sew top and bottom borders to wall hanging. Sew side borders to wall hanging to complete **Wall Hanging Top**.

Wall Hanging Top

7. Follow **Assembling The Quilt**, pg. 155, to layer backing, fleece, and wall hanging top and to baste all layers together.

8. Follow **Quilting**, pg. 156, and stitch wall hanging in the ditch along all seamlines. Trim fleece and backing even with edges of wall hanging.

9. Follow **Making Continuous Bias Strip Binding**, pg. 156, and use a 27″ square to make 5 yds of 2¹/₂″w binding.

10. Follow **Attaching Binding With Mitered Corners**, pg. 157, and attach bias binding to wall hanging.

11. Refer to **Making A Hanging Sleeve**, pg. 158, to make and attach hanging sleeve to back of wall hanging.

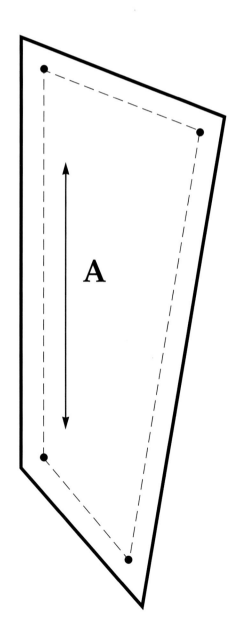

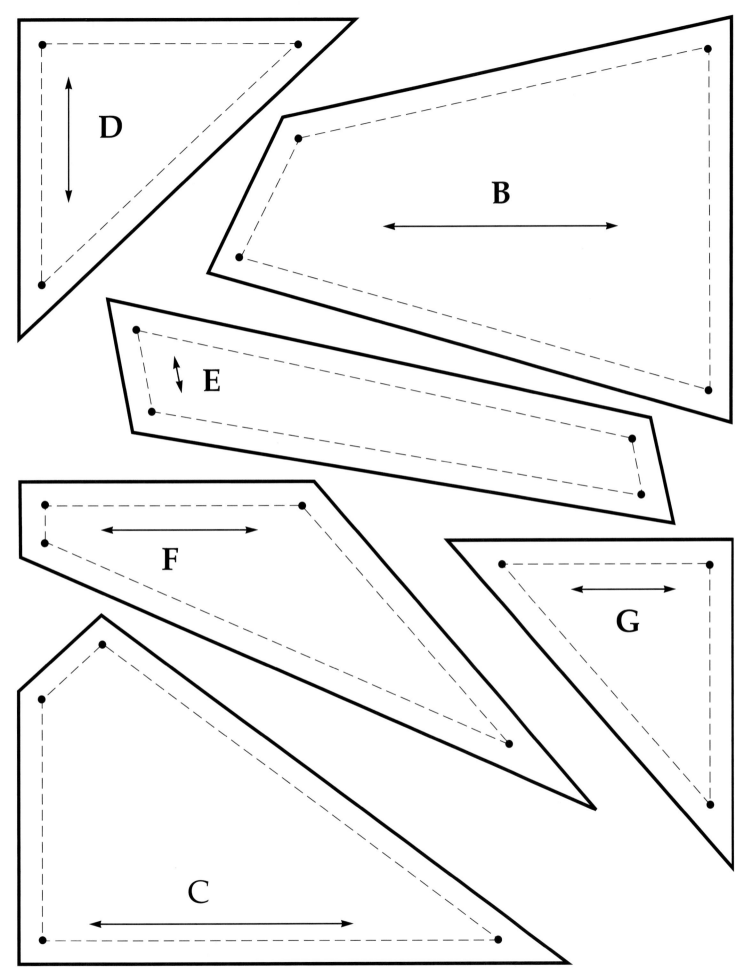

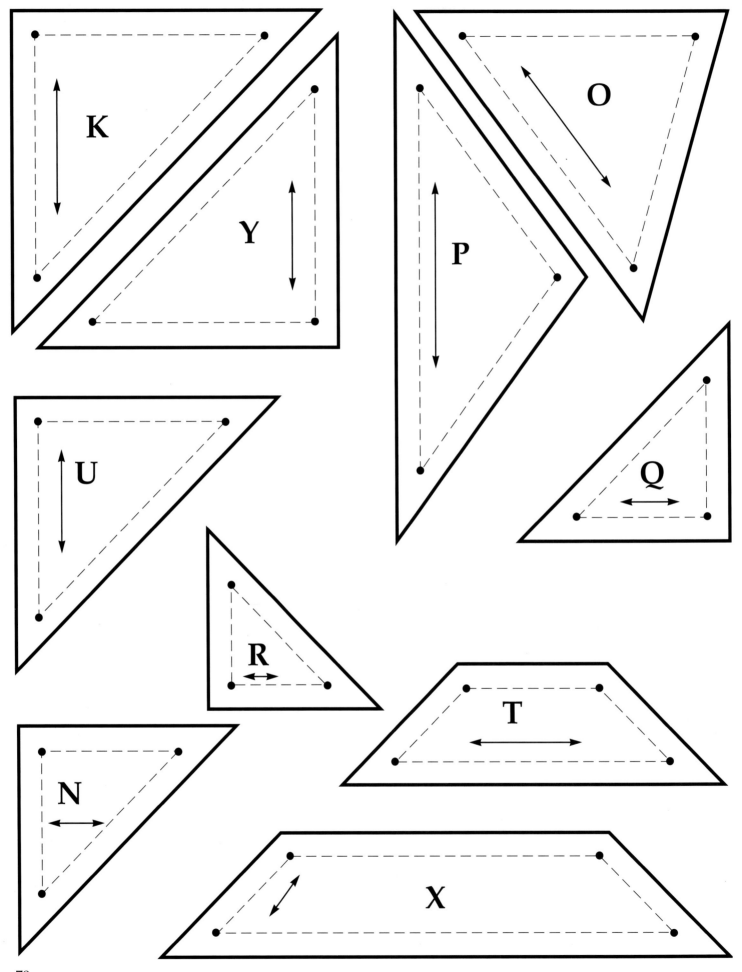

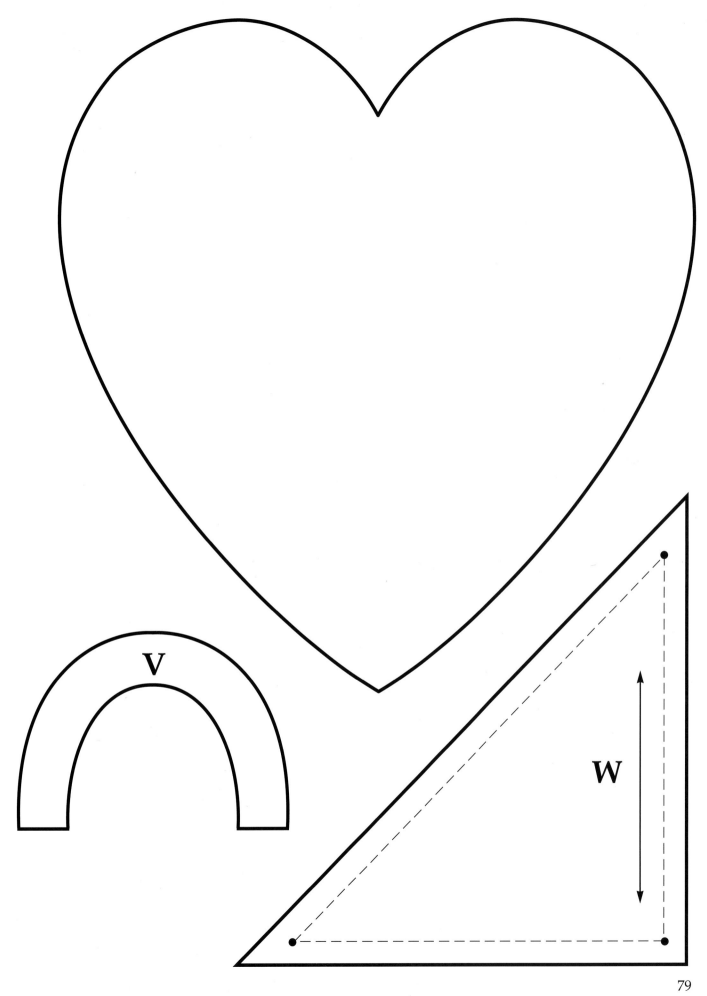

V

W

NEW YORK BEAUTY

Today, as in years past, the completion of a New York Beauty quilt is a milestone achievement for a quilter. A bold combination of curves and triangles makes the quilt a masterpiece of stitching talent and creativity. Popularly known as Rocky Mountain Road or Crown of Thorns in the 1800's, the pattern was renamed early in the 1900's. The curving strips of white triangles could be seen as symbolic of the Statue of Liberty's crown, an emblem of hope for many new immigrants to America. For a pretty finish, the antique quilt shown here features an inner border of green and an outer border of white triangles and pink teardrops.

NEW YORK BEAUTY

Size
Block: 15¾" x 15¾"
Quilt: 93" x 93"

Yardage Requirements
Ecru fabric — 7½ yds of 45"w
Pink fabric — 6 yds of 45"w
Green fabric — 2¾ yds of 45"w
Binding — 1 yd of 45"w pink fabric
Backing — 8⅝ yds of 45"w **OR** 2⅞ yds of 108"w
120" x 120" piece of low-loft polyester bonded
  batting

Cutting Out Pieces
1. Follow **Making Templates**, pg. 147, to make
   templates from all pattern pieces on pgs. 84-85.
2. To complete our quilt you will need 16 blocks.
   Follow **Cutting Out Quilt Pieces**, pg. 147, and
   cut out the following:
   A — 576 from pink fabric
   B — 512 from ecru fabric
   C — 64 from green fabric
   D — 64 from pink fabric
   E — 16 from ecru fabric
   F — 952 from ecru fabric
   F — 1004 from pink fabric
   G — 24 (2½" x 16¼") pieces of green fabric
   H — 9 from pink fabric
   I — 36 from ecru fabric
   J — 36 from green fabric
   K — 4 from ecru fabric
   L — 2 (2½" x 81½") pieces from green fabric
   M — 2 (2½" x 85½") pieces from green fabric
   N — 136 from ecru fabric
   O — 144 from pink fabric

Assembling The Quilt
1. For each block, follow **Piecing And Pressing**,
   pg. 148, and sew 8 **B's** between 9 **A's** to make
   Unit 1. Repeat to make a total of 4 **Unit 1's**.

Unit 1

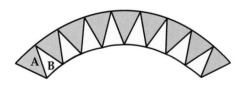

2. Follow **Sewing Curves**, pg. 150, and sew
   1 **Unit 1** to 1 **C** to make **Unit 2**. Repeat to make a
   total of 4 **Unit 2's**.

Unit 2

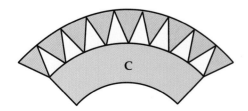

3. Sew 1 **Unit 2** to 1 **D** to make **Unit 3**. Repeat to
   make a total of 4 **Unit 3's**. Trim outer straight
   edge of triangles on **Unit 3's** even with edges of
   C and **D**.

Unit 3

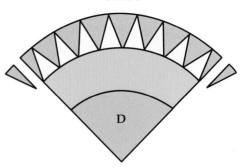

4. Sew 4 **Unit 3's** to 1 **E** to complete block.

Block

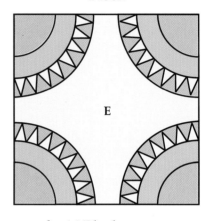

5. Repeat to make 16 **Blocks**.
6. For sashing, sew 14 ecru **F's** between 15 pink **F's**
   to make **Unit 4**. Repeat to make a total of
   48 **Unit 4's**.

Unit 4

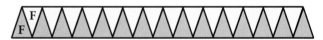

7. Sew 1 **G** between 2 **Unit 4's** to make **Unit 5**.
   Repeat to make a total of 24 **Unit 5's**. Trim
   triangles on **Unit 5's** even with edges of **G**.

Unit 5

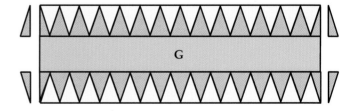

8. For setting squares, sew 1 **I** between 2 **J's** to make **Unit 6**. Repeat to make a total of 18 **Unit 6's**. Sew 1 **H** between 2 **I's** to make **Unit 7**. Repeat to make a total of 9 **Unit 7's**. Sew 1 **Unit 7** between 2 **Unit 6's** to make **Unit 8**. Repeat to make a total of 9 **Unit 8's**.

Unit 6   **Unit 7**   **Unit 8**

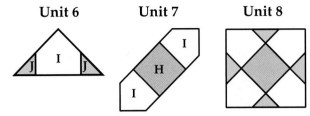

9. Sew 3 **Unit 5's** between 4 **Blocks** to make **Row 1**. Repeat to make **Rows 2-4**.

Row 1

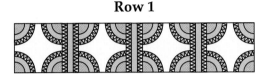

10. Sew 3 **Unit 8's** between 4 **Unit 5's** to make **Unit 9**. Repeat to make a total of 3 **Unit 9's**.

Unit 9

11. Sew 1 **Unit 9** between **Row 1** and **Row 2**. Repeat to add **Rows 3** and **4** and remaining **Unit 9's** to complete **Quilt Top**.

Quilt Top

12. For inner pieced border, sew 70 ecru **F's** between 71 pink **F's** beginning and ending with a pink **F**. Repeat to make a total of 4 pieced borders. Square each end of pieced borders by trimming off ½ of the beginning and ending **F** triangles.

13. Matching ecru triangles to quilt top, sew 1 pieced border each to top and bottom of quilt top.

14. Sew 2 **K's** and 1 **L** to 1 remaining pieced border to make **Unit 10**. Repeat to make a total of 2 **Unit 10's**.

Unit 10

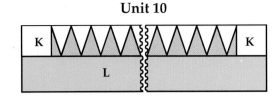

15. Matching pieced border to quilt top, sew 1 **Unit 10** to each side of quilt top.

16. Sew 1 **M** each to top and bottom of quilt top.

17. For outer pieced borders, sew 34 **N's** between 35 **O's** beginning and ending with an **O**, to make **Unit 11**. Repeat to make a total of 4 **Unit 11's**.

Unit 11

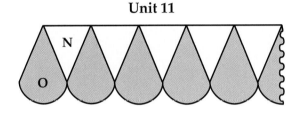

18. Sew 1 outer pieced border each to top, bottom, and sides of quilt top. Follow **Sewing Into A Corner**, pg. 150, and sew 1 **O** into each corner of outer pieced border *(Fig. 1)*.

Fig. 1

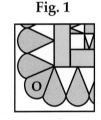

19. Follow **Marking Quilting Lines**, pg. 154, and **Quilting Diagram** and **Quilting Pattern**, pg. 85, to mark quilting lines on quilt top.

Quilting Diagram

20. To piece backing if necessary, cut fabric into 3 (2⁷/₈) yd pieces. Matching right sides and long edges and using a ¹/₄" seam allowance, sew pieces together along long edges. Press seam allowances open.

21. Follow **Assembling The Quilt**, pg. 155, to layer backing, batting, and quilt top and to baste all layers together.

22. Follow **Quilting**, pg. 156, and stitch quilt along marked lines. Trim batting and backing even with edges of quilt.

23. Follow **Steps 1-7** of **Making Continuous Bias Strip Binding**, pg. 156, and use a 36" square to make an 18 yd length of 1¹/₄"w bias binding.

24. Press one long edge of bias binding ¹/₄" to wrong side. Press one short end of bias binding ¹/₂" to wrong side. Matching right sides and raw edges and beginning with pressed end, sew binding to quilt using a ¹/₄" seam allowance. Fold binding over to quilt backing and pin pressed edge in place, covering stitching line. Blind stitch binding to backing.

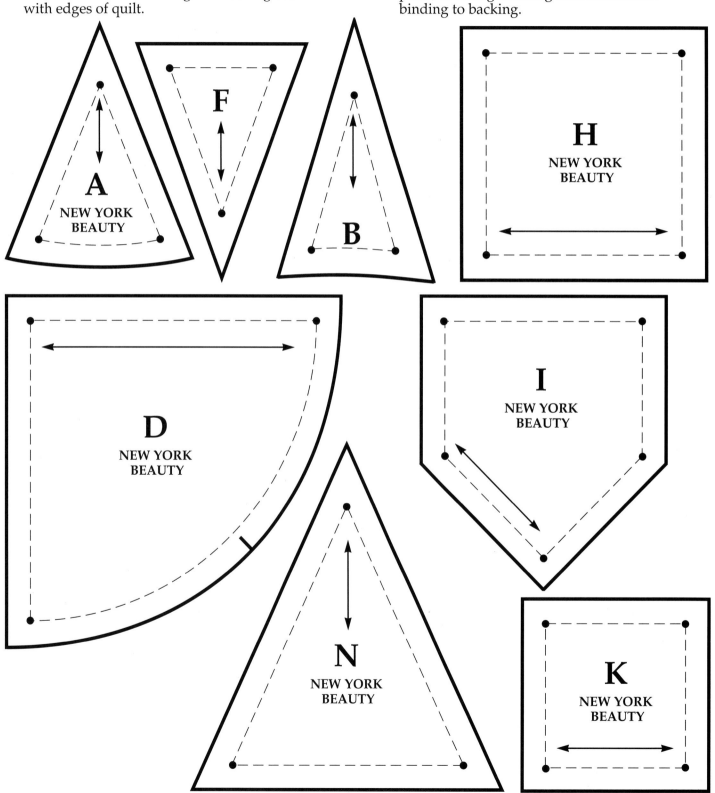

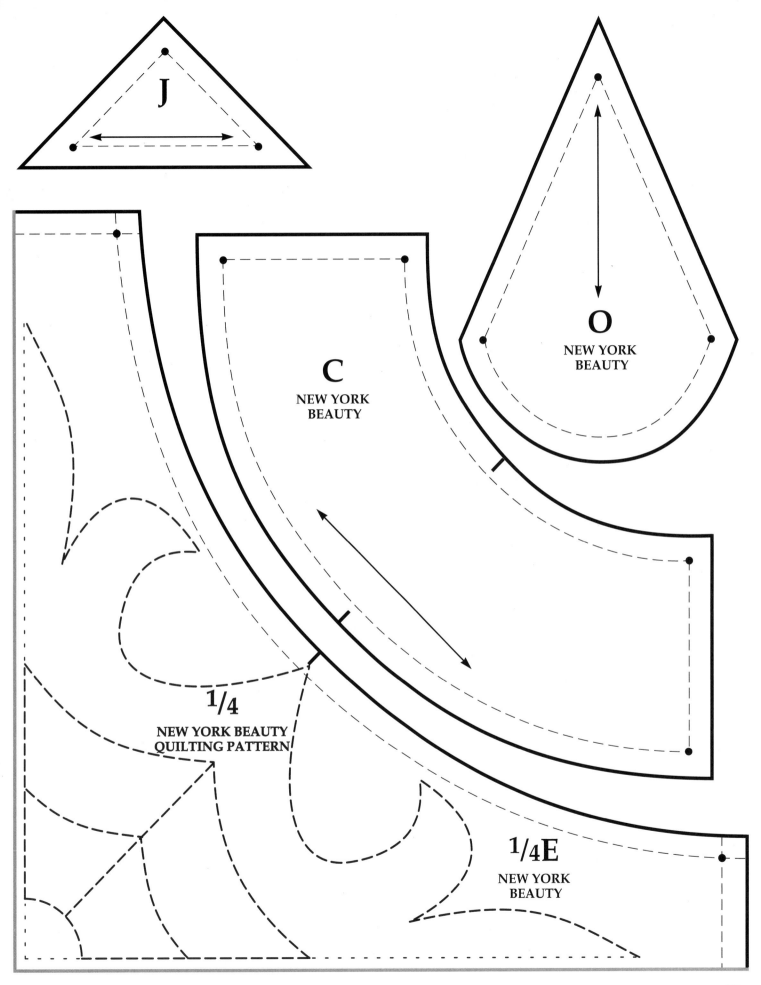

J

O

NEW YORK
BEAUTY

C

NEW YORK
BEAUTY

1/4

NEW YORK BEAUTY
QUILTING PATTERN

1/4E

NEW YORK
BEAUTY

85

BEAR'S PAW COLLECTION

Long before the popularity of President Theodore Roosevelt inspired the lovable, huggable teddy bear, pioneer women immortalized the furry creature with the Bear's Paw quilt pattern. Red and white was a favorite color scheme for this classic design, which is created with a combination of squares and triangles. Also known by such picturesque names as Hands all Around and Duck's Foot in the Mud, the pattern was common in many areas of the United States. The striking quilt shown here in a rustic setting will bring a touch of Americana to any decor.

Traditional Bear's Paw blocks add country charm to an ordinary sweatshirt. These adorable child's overalls, featuring a lovable bear face, are created by adding a handmade bib and cuffs to purchased trousers.

(Opposite) An old-fashioned jointed teddy bear is the focus of the coordinating wall hanging. The corner blocks are pieced, and the bear is appliquéd by hand.

89

BEAR'S PAW QUILT

Size
Block: 11¾" x 11¾"
Quilt: 82" x 91"

Yardage Requirements
Ecru fabric — 5¼ yds of 45"w
Red fabric — 2½ yds of 45"w
Binding — 1⅛ yd of 45"w red fabric
Backing — 5½ yds of 45"w **OR** 2¾ yds of 90"w
90" x 108" piece of low-loft polyester bonded
batting

Cutting Out Pieces
1. Follow **Making Templates**, pg. 147, to make templates from patterns **A-D** on pg. 95.
2. To complete our quilt you will need 20 blocks. Follow **Cutting Out Quilt Pieces**, pg. 147, and cut out the following:
   Inner borders — 2 (2" x 68") pieces of red fabric
   Inner borders — 2 (2" x 82¼") pieces of red fabric
   Outer borders — 2 (7¼" x 63") pieces of ecru fabric
   Outer borders — 2 (9¾" x 90¾") pieces of ecru fabric
   Sashing — 49 (3" x 12¼") pieces of ecru fabric
   Setting squares — 30 (3") squares of red fabric
   A — 320 from ecru fabric
   A — 320 from red fabric
   B — 80 from ecru fabric
   B — 20 from red fabric
   C — 80 from red fabric
   D — 80 from ecru fabric

Assembling The Quilt
1. For each block, follow **Piecing And Pressing**, pg. 148, and **Unit 1** diagram to sew pieces together to make **Unit 1**. Repeat to make a total of 4 **Unit 1's**.

Unit 1

2. Follow **Unit 2** diagram and sew pieces together to make **Unit 2**. Repeat to make a total of 4 **Unit 2's**.

Unit 2

3. Sew 1 **Unit 1** to 1 **Unit 2** to make **Unit 3**. Repeat to make a total of 4 **Unit 3's**.

Unit 3

4. Sew 1 **D** between 2 **Unit 3's** to make **Unit 4.** Repeat to make a total of 2 **Unit 4's**. Sew 1 red **B** between 2 **D's** to make **Unit 5.**

Unit 4

Unit 5
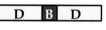

5. Sew **Unit 5** between 2 **Unit 4's** to complete **Block.**

Block

6. Repeat to make 20 **Blocks**.
7. Sew 4 **Blocks** between 5 sashing strips to make **Row 1**. Repeat to make **Rows 2-5**.

Row 1
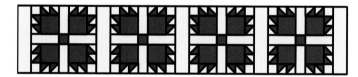

8. Sew 4 sashing strips between 5 setting squares to make **Unit 6**. Repeat to make a total of 6 **Unit 6's**.

Unit 6

9. Sew **Row 1** between 2 **Unit 6's**. Repeat to add **Rows 2-5** and remaining **Unit 6's** to complete **Quilt Top**.

Quilt Top

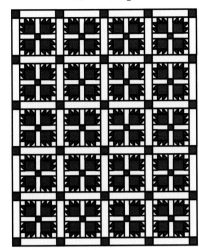

10. Follow **Adding Mitered Borders**, pg. 153, and add inner borders.
11. For outer borders, sew 63" strips to top and bottom of quilt top. Sew 90³/4" strips to sides of quilt top.
12. Follow **Marking Quilting Lines**, pg. 154, and **Quilting Diagram** and **Quilting Pattern**, pg. 96, to mark quilting lines on quilt top.

Quilting Diagram

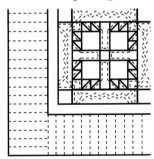

13. Follow **Preparing Backing And Batting**, pg. 155, to piece backing if necessary.
14. Follow **Assembling The Quilt**, pg. 155, to layer backing, batting, and quilt top and to baste all layers together.
15. Follow **Quilting**, pg. 156, and stitch quilt along marked lines. Trim batting and backing even with edges of quilt.
16. Follow **Making Continuous Bias Strip Binding**, pg. 156, and use a 36" square to make 10¹/2 yds of 2¹/2"w bias binding.
17. Follow **Attaching Binding With Mitered Corners**, pg. 157, and attach bias binding to quilt.

APPLIQUÉD SWEATSHIRT
Approx. Design Size: 23"w x 6³/8"h

Supplies
Purchased sweatshirt with set-in sleeves
3" square of medium fabric #1
1/4 yd of 45"w medium fabric #2
6" x 18" piece of light fabric
6" x 18" piece of dark fabric
1 yd of paper-backed fusible web
Tear-away fabric stabilizer **OR** freezer paper
Clear thread for zigzag stitching
Sewing thread for piecing
Tracing paper
Seam ripper

Instructions
1. Wash, dry, and press sweatshirt and fabrics.
2. Trace patterns **E** and **F** on pg. 95. Cut out patterns.
3. Follow manufacturer's instructions to fuse paper-backed fusible web to wrong side of dark fabric and medium fabric #1. Do **not** remove paper backing at this time.
4. To complete sweatshirt, cut out the following:
   E — 12 from dark fabric
   F — 3 from medium fabric #1
   G — 3 (5¹/2") squares from light fabric
   H — 2 (1⁵/8" x 5¹/2") pieces from medium fabric #2
   I — 2 (3¹/2" x 5¹/2") pieces from medium fabric #2
   J — Measure front of sweatshirt from armhole to armhole 2" below neckband **(Fig. 1)**. Add 1/2" to measurement to allow for seam allowances. Cut 2 pieces 1¹/4" by determined measurement from medium fabric #2.

Fig. 1

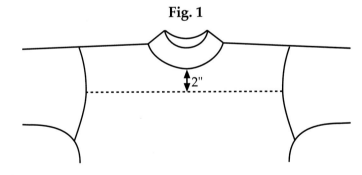

5. *Note: Use ¹/4" seam allowance for all seams.* Sew 2 **H's** between 3 **G's** to make **Unit 1**. Sew 1 **I** to each end of **Unit 1** to make **Unit 2**. Press seam allowances open.

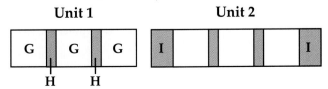

Unit 1   Unit 2

6. Press 1 long edge of each **J** ¼" to wrong side. Matching right sides and raw edges, sew **Unit 2** between **J's** to make **Unit 3**.

Unit 3

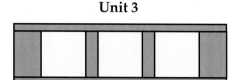

7. Remove paper backing from **E's** and **F's**. Refer to photo for placement and follow manufacturer's instructions to fuse **E's** and **F's** to **G's**. Use clear thread to zigzag stitch along raw edges of **E's** and **F's**.

8. Cut a piece of paper-backed fusible web slightly smaller than **Unit 3**. Fuse web to wrong side of **Unit 3**. Remove paper backing.

9. Center **Unit 3** on front of sweatshirt 2" below neckband with edges extending over armhole seams. Use seam ripper to open armhole seams as far as necessary to insert **Unit 3** into seams. Trim edges even with armhole seams. Fuse **Unit 3** to shirt.

10. Cut a piece of fabric stabilizer or freezer paper slightly larger than **Unit 3**. Baste stabilizer or iron freezer paper to wrong side of shirt under **Unit 3**. Sew **Unit 3** to shirt by topstitching along each long edge of **H's**, **I's**, and **J's**. Remove stabilizer; knot and trim thread ends.

11. Sew armhole seams closed.

BEAR OVERALLS

Supplies

Children's pants (photo model Boys size 6-7)
½ yd of 45"w medium fabric #1 for bib, straps, and cuffs
6" square of light fabric for outer ears
6½" square of light fabric for head
2½" square of white fabric for eyes
2½" square of black fabric for eyes and nose
5" square of medium fabric #2 for muzzle and inner ears
8" x 10" piece of fusible interfacing
½ yd of paper-backed fusible web
5 — ⅝" buttons
Thread to match appliqué fabrics
Tracing paper

Instructions

1. Wash, dry, and press pants and fabrics.
2. Trace patterns **K-Q** on pgs. 95-96. Cut out patterns.
3. Follow manufacturer's instructions to fuse paper-backed fusible web to wrong side of light fabric for head, white fabric, black fabric, and medium fabric #2. Do **not** remove paper backing at this time.

4. To complete project, cut out the following:
   K — 1 from light fabric
   L — 4 from light fabric
   M — 2 (1 in reverse) from white fabric
   N — 2 (1 in reverse) from black fabric
   O — 1 from black fabric
   P —1 from medium fabric #2
   Q — 2 from medium fabric #2
   Bib — 2 (8" x 10") pieces from medium fabric #1
   Straps — 2 (3¾" x 25") pieces from medium fabric #1
5. Remove paper backing and lightly trace detail lines onto appliqué pieces.
6. Follow manufacturer's instructions to fuse interfacing to wrong side of 1 bib piece. This will be bib front.
7. Fuse 1 inner ear to right side of 1 outer ear. Repeat with remaining inner ear and outer ear. Refer to **Machine Appliqué**, pg. 152, to appliqué inner ears to outer ears. With right sides together, sew remaining outer ears to appliquéd outer ears. Clip curves and turn right side out; press.
8. With short edges of bib at top and bottom, refer to photo for placement and place appliqué pieces on right side of bib front, slipping ears under edge of head. Fuse head to bib.
9. Machine appliqué pieces to bib and stitch muzzle and eyebrow detail and highlight in eyes. (Curved edges of ears are **not** appliquéd, leaving them free for a 3-D effect.)
10. Press lower edge of bib front ½" to wrong side. Press 1 short edge of bib back ½" to wrong side. Matching right sides and raw edges, sew bib front to bib back along both long edges and unpressed short edge using a ½" seam allowance. Trim corners diagonally and turn right side out; press. Hand sew opening closed.
11. Make buttonholes in bib as indicated in **Fig. 2**. Position lower edge of bib inside front of pants waistband to determine position of buttons. Sew buttons to inside of waistband. Button bib onto waistband.

Fig. 2

12. Matching right sides and long raw edges, fold each strap in half. Sew long edge and 1 short edge using a ½" seam allowance. Turn right side out; press. Sew ends of straps to inside back waistband of pants. Try pants on child. Adjust strap length to fit child and sew button to each strap.

13. The pant cuffs are made by fusing fabric directly to the wrong side of the pant legs. To make cuff pattern, lay pant leg on tracing paper with seams at each side and use a pencil to draw across bottom of pant leg and 4¾" along each side seam. Remove pant leg and connect the top of each side seam pencil line. Add ½" to all edges. Use pattern to cut 4 cuffs (2 in reverse) from medium fabric #1. Matching right sides, sew 2 cuff pieces together along sides using ½" seam allowance. Repeat for remaining cuff. Press seams open. Press top and bottom edges of cuffs ½" to wrong side. Cut paper-backed fusible web the size of each cuff. Fuse web to wrong side of each cuff. Remove paper backing. Matching wrong side of each cuff to wrong side of each pant leg, fuse cuffs to pant legs. Roll up cuffs as desired.

WALL HANGING

Size
32" x 32"

Supplies
Ecru fabric — ¼ yd of 45"w
Floral fabric — 14" x 11" piece
Large check fabric — 14" x 5" piece
Small check fabric (includes binding) — ⅞ yd of 45"w
Red fabric — ⅝ yd of 45"w
Brown fabric for bear — ⅜ yd of 45"w
Tan fabric for muzzle and ears — 5" square
Backing and hanging sleeve — ⅞ yd of 45"w fabric
38" x 38" piece of fleece
2 — ⅝" buttons for joints
2 — snaps for eyes
Embroidery floss — black and tan
Thread to match fabrics
Dressmaker's tracing paper and tracing wheel

Cutting Out The Pieces
1. Follow **Making Templates**, pg. 147, to make templates from patterns **R-U** and **CC-FF** on pgs. 96-97. (*Note: Patterns for appliqué templates CC-FF do not include seam allowances; add seam allowances to these pieces when they are cut out.*)
2. Follow **Cutting Out Quilt Pieces**, pg. 147, and cut out the following:
   R — 64 from ecru fabric
   R — 64 from red fabric

S — 16 from ecru fabric
S — 4 from small check fabric
T — 16 from red fabric
U — 16 from ecru fabric
V — 8 (14½" x 3½") pieces of red fabric
W — 4 (14½" x 1½") pieces of ecru fabric
W — 2 (14½" x 1½") pieces of small check fabric
X — 1 (12½" x 9½") piece of floral fabric
Y — 1 (12½" x 3½") piece of large check fabric
Z — 2 (12" x 1½") pieces of small check fabric
AA — 2 (28½" x 2½") pieces of small check fabric
BB — 2 (32" x 2½") pieces of small check fabric
CC — 1 from tan fabric
DD — 1 from red fabric
EE — 1 from brown fabric
FF — 2 (1 in reverse) from tan fabric
Binding — 2 (32" x 2") and 2 (33" x 2") pieces from small check fabric

Assembling The Wall Hanging
1. Follow **Steps 1-5** of **Bear's Paw Quilt**, substituting patterns **R-U** for **A-D** to make 4 blocks.
2. Sew 1 ecru **W** between 2 **V's** to make **Unit 1**. Repeat to make a total of 4 **Unit 1's**.

Unit 1

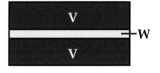

3. Follow **Unit 2** diagram and sew pieces together to make **Unit 2**.

Unit 2

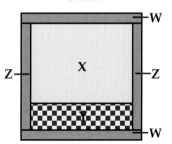

4. Sew **Unit 2** between 2 **Unit 1's** to make **Unit 3**.

Unit 3

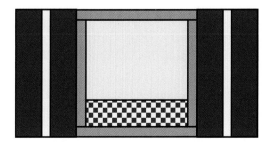

5. Sew 1 **Unit 1** between 2 completed blocks to make **Unit 4**. Repeat to make a total of 2 **Unit 4's**.

Unit 4

6. Sew **Unit 3** between 2 **Unit 4's** to make **Unit 5**.

Unit 5

7. Sew 2 **AA's** and 2 **BB's** to **Unit 5** to complete **Wall Hanging Background**.

Wall Hanging Background

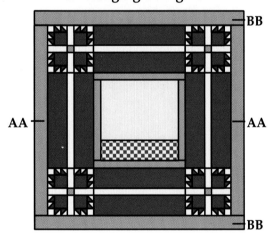

8. Use dressmaker's tracing paper and tracing wheel to transfer detail lines (indicated by dashed lines on pattern) to right side of bear appliqué. Transfer detail lines to right side of muzzle appliqué.
9. Refer to photo for placement and follow **Hand Appliqué**, pg. 151, to appliqué bear to background. Appliqué ears, muzzle, and heart to bear.

10. Use 4 strands of floss for all embroidery stitches. Use tan floss and **Outline Stitch**, pg. 159, to embroider detail lines on bear. Use black floss and **Outline Stitch** to embroider detail lines on muzzle. Use black floss and **Satin Stitch**, pg. 159, to embroider nose on muzzle.
11. Refer to photo for placement and sew buttons and snaps to bear.
12. Refer to **Marking Quilting Lines**, pg. 154, and **Quilting Diagram** to mark quilting lines.

Quilting Diagram

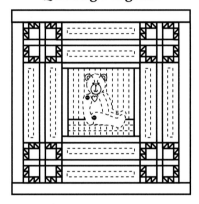

13. Follow **Assembling The Quilt**, pg. 155, to layer backing, fleece, and wall hanging top and to baste all layers together.
14. Follow **Quilting**, pg. 156, and stitch wall hanging in the ditch along all seamlines and along all marked lines.
15. Fold each piece of binding in half, matching wrong sides and long edges; press along fold. Matching right sides and raw edges and using a 1/2" seam allowance, sew 1 (32") piece of binding to each side of wall hanging. Fold binding over to quilt backing and pin pressed edge in place, covering stitching line. Blind stitch binding to backing.
16. With ends of binding extending 1/2" beyond wall hanging on each side, match right sides and raw edges and use a 1/2" seam allowance to sew 1 (33") piece of binding each to top and bottom of wall hanging. Press short ends of binding 1/2" to wrong side. Fold binding over to quilt backing and pin pressed edge in place, covering stitching line. Blind stitch binding to backing.
17. Refer to **Making Hanging Sleeve**, pg. 158, to make and attach hanging sleeve to back of wall hanging.

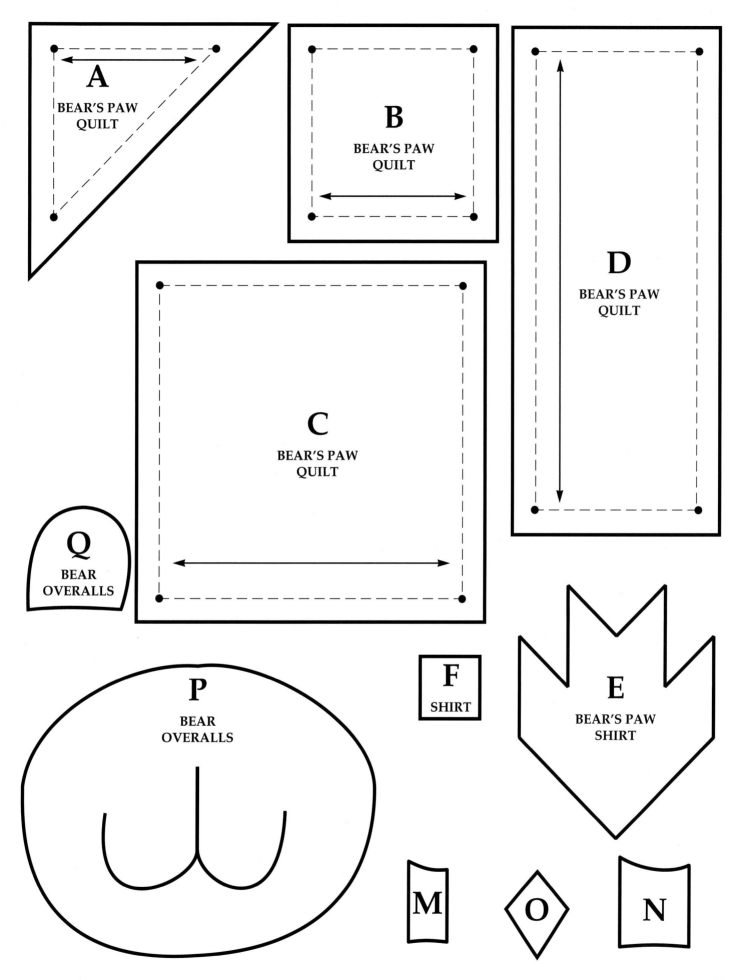

A
BEAR'S PAW
QUILT

B
BEAR'S PAW
QUILT

D
BEAR'S PAW
QUILT

C
BEAR'S PAW
QUILT

Q
BEAR
OVERALLS

P
BEAR
OVERALLS

F
SHIRT

E
BEAR'S PAW
SHIRT

M

O

N

95

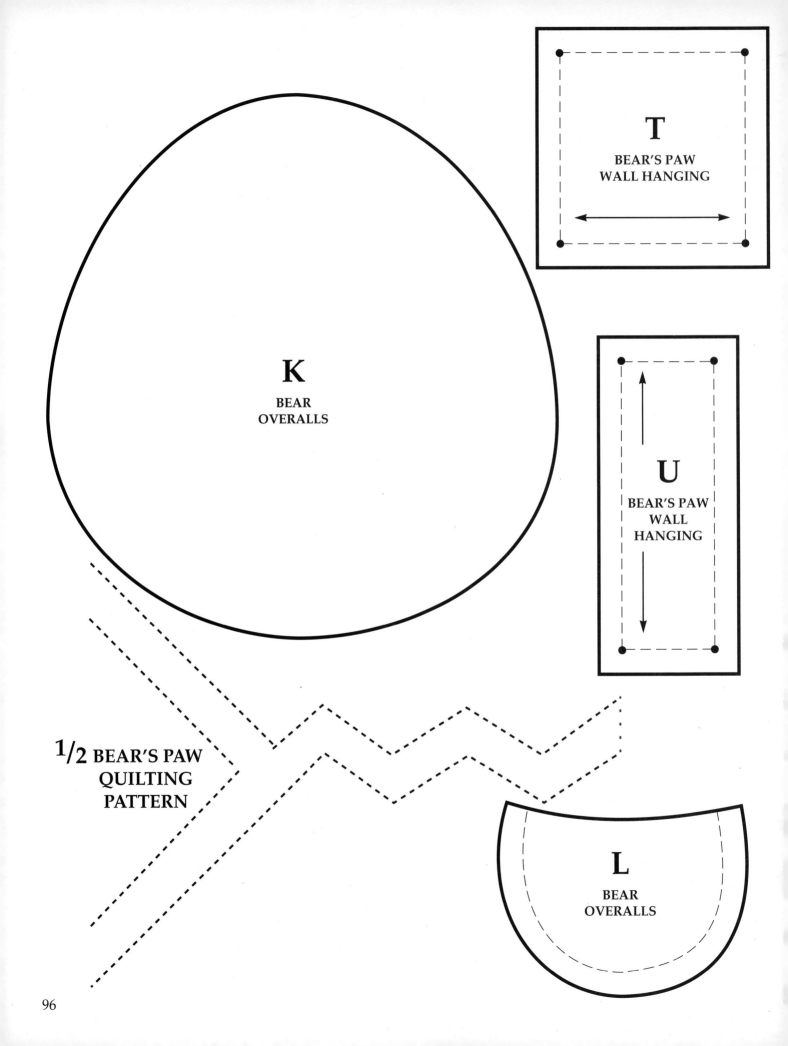

T

BEAR'S PAW
WALL HANGING

U

BEAR'S PAW
WALL
HANGING

K

BEAR
OVERALLS

L

BEAR
OVERALLS

**1/2 BEAR'S PAW
QUILTING
PATTERN**

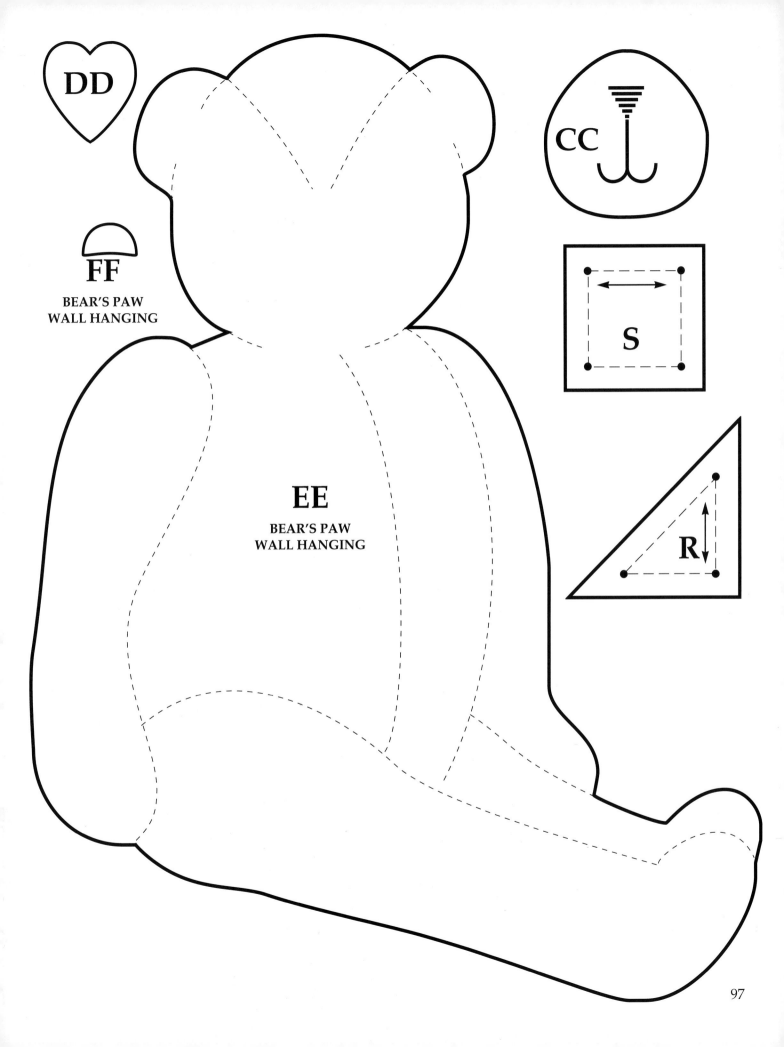

DD

CC

FF

BEAR'S PAW
WALL HANGING

S

EE

BEAR'S PAW
WALL HANGING

R

ALBUM QUILT

The rich heritage of the Album quilt can be traced back to the pioneer days of America. Sometimes given as friendship quilts, Album quilts were usually presented to departing families as a pretty (but practical) remembrance of those left behind. The women of the community would each piece a block for the quilt and then gather for a quilting bee to see it finished. Especially during the mid to late 1800's when autograph albums were popular, each woman would sign the center of her block and embroider over the signature (see our pillow on page 141). Pieced from familiar fabrics that stirred memories of loved ones, these quilts became known as ''albums.'' The antique quilt shown here was left unsigned, evidence of how some quilters appreciated the beauty of the pattern on its own. Its rich fall colors bring to mind images of autumn's annual blanket of leaves.

ALBUM QUILT

Size
Block: 13" x 13"
Quilt: 73" x 87"

Yardage Requirements
Ecru fabric — 2⅞ yds of 45"w
Assorted dark fabrics — total of 2¼ yds of 45"w
Brown fabric — 2⅞ yds of 45"w
Binding — ⅞ yd of 45"w
Backing — 5¼ yds of 45"w **OR** 2⅝ yds of 90"w
81" x 96" piece of low-loft polyester bonded batting

Cutting Out Pieces
1. Follow **Making Templates**, pg. 147, to make templates from all patterns on pg. 101.
2. To complete our quilt you will need 30 blocks. Follow **Cutting Out Quilt Pieces**, pg. 147, and cut out the following:
   Sashing — 49 (2¼" x 14") pieces from ecru fabric
   Setting squares — 20 (2¼") squares from brown fabric
   A — 30 from ecru fabric
   A — 120 from assorted dark fabrics
   B — 60 from ecru fabric
   B — 240 from assorted dark fabrics
   C — 360 from ecru fabric
   D — 120 from ecru fabric
   E — 60 (2¼" x 10½") pieces from brown fabric
   F — 60 (2¼" x 14") pieces from brown fabric

Assembling The Quilt
1. For each block, follow **Piecing And Pressing**, pg. 148, and **Unit 1** diagram to sew pieces together to make **Unit 1**. Sew **Unit 1** between 2 dark fabric **A's** to make **Unit 2**.

Unit 1   **Unit 2**

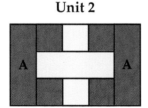

2. Follow **Unit 3** diagram and sew pieces together to make **Unit 3**. Repeat to make a total of 4 **Unit 3's**. Sew 1 dark fabric **A** between 2 **C's** to make **Unit 4**. Repeat to make a total of 2 **Unit 4's**.

Unit 3   **Unit 4**

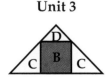 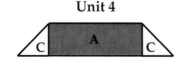

3. Follow **Unit 5** diagram and sew **Unit 3's** and **Unit 4's** to **Unit 2** to make **Unit 5**.

Unit 5

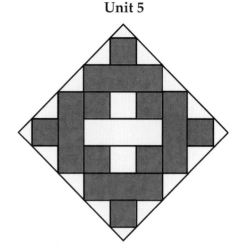

4. Sew **Unit 5** between 2 **E's** to make **Unit 6**.

Unit 6

5. Sew **Unit 6** between 2 **F's** to complete **Block**.

Block

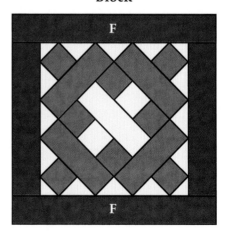

6. Repeat to make 30 **Blocks**.
7. Sew 4 sashing strips between 5 **Blocks** to make **Row 1**. Repeat to make **Rows 2-6**.

Row 1

8. Sew 4 setting squares between 5 sashing strips to make **Unit 7**. Repeat to make a total of 5 **Unit 7's**.

Unit 7

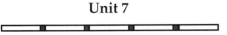

9. Sew 1 **Unit 7** between **Row 1** and **Row 2**. Repeat to add **Rows 3-6** and remaining **Unit 7's** to complete **Quilt Top**.

Quilt Top

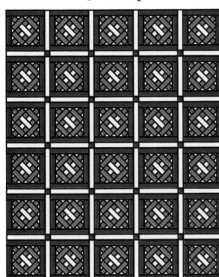

10. Follow **Marking Quilting Lines**, pg. 154, and **Quilting Diagram** to mark quilting lines on quilt top.

Quilting Diagram

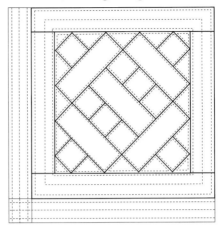

11. Follow **Preparing Backing And Batting**, pg. 155, to piece backing if necessary.
12. Follow **Assembling The Quilt**, pg. 155, to layer backing, batting, and quilt top and to baste all layers together.
13. Follow **Quilting**, pg. 156, and stitch quilt along marked lines. Trim batting and backing even with edges of quilt.
14. Follow **Making Continuous Bias Strip Binding**, pg. 156, and use a 27" square to make 10 yds of 2"w bias binding.
15. Follow **Attaching Binding With Mitered Corners**, pg. 157, and attach bias binding to quilt.

B
ALBUM
QUILT

C
ALBUM
QUILT

D

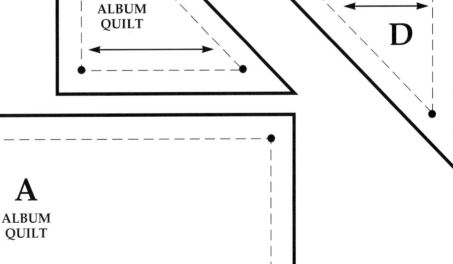

A
ALBUM
QUILT

SUNNY GARDEN

Bold, bright sunflowers have long been a favorite of gardeners and quilters alike. A dramatic sight in many flower gardens, the giant golden blooms lend themselves well to quilted creations. Blocks of an old-fashioned Sunflower quilt pattern were incorporated into this modern wall hanging, with charming results. Made with a combination of piecework and appliqué, the garden scene features a lively blend of fabrics in prints, plaids, checks, and solids. Inspired by this sunny piece, we created the fun clothing items shown on the following pages.

Blackbirds and sunflowers adorn these cute country wearables. The jacket is trimmed with blanket stitching and appliquéd with blackbirds and a showy three-dimensional sunflower. More appliquéd blackbirds and golden Yo-Yo flowers dress up a rugged shirt; checked fabric trims complete the look. Inquisitive stuffed blackbirds with button-jointed wings make cute decorations for your home.

APPLIQUÉD JACKET

Supplies

Denim jacket with pockets
Brown fabric for birds — 8" square
Tan fabric for stems and flower — 1/8 yd of 45"w
Brown fabric for flower center — 5" square
Green fabric for large leaves — 6" square
Assorted green fabric for small leaves — 5 (2")
  squares
Paper-backed fusible web — 1/4 yd
1/8" double-face satin ribbon — 1/2 yd
Six strand embroidery floss — black and tan
Thread to match ribbon and tan fabric
Quilting thread

Instructions

1. Trace patterns **A-D** on pgs. 109-111. Cut out patterns.
2. Follow manufacturer's instructions to fuse paper-backed fusible web to wrong side of brown fabric (for birds) and green fabric. Do **not** remove paper backing at this time.
3. To complete project, cut out the following:
   A — 2 from brown fabric
   B — 2 from green fabric
   C — 4 from green fabric
   D — 1 from green fabric
   E — 1 (4" x 24") piece from tan fabric
   F — 1 (3½") circle from brown fabric
   Stems — 1 (1½" x 8") and 1 (1½" x 5") piece

Assembling The Jacket

1. Matching wrong sides and long edges, fold each stem in half; press. Fold raw edges of each stem to center and press. Refer to photo for placement and **Hand Appliqué**, pg. 151, to appliqué stems to jacket. Drape ribbon around stems and tack to jacket.
2. Remove paper backing from appliqués. Refer to photo for placement and follow manufacturer's instructions to fuse birds and leaves to jacket. Use 3 strands of black floss to **Blanket Stitch** (pg. 159) around appliqué pieces.
3. For ruched flower, press short ends of **E** ½" to wrong side. Matching wrong sides and long edges, fold **E** in half; press. Mark strip as shown in **Fig. 1**. Using quilting thread, baste along marked lines. Pull basting thread drawing fabric strip up as tightly as possible to form a circle; knot and clip ends of thread. Sew short ends together. Refer to photo for placement and sew flower to jacket.

Fig. 1

4. Appliqué **F** to center of flower.

5. Use 6 strands of tan floss to **Blanket Stitch** lapels and fronts of jacket.

APPLIQUÉD SHIRT

Supplies

Cape front shirt (*Note: If cape front shirt is not available, design may be placed on any shirt without pockets.*)
Black check fabric for birds, binding, collar and cuffs — 1/2 yd of 45"w
Tan fabric for binding — 3/8 yd of 45"w
Green fabric for leaves and stems — 6" square
Black fabric for wings — 4" square
Assorted fabrics for yo-yo flowers — 4 (3") circles
Scrap of gold fabric for beaks
Paper-backed fusible web — 1/4 yd
4 shank-style buttons for flower centers
Black six strand embroidery floss

Instructions

1. Trace patterns **A** and **G-J** on pgs. 110-111. Cut out patterns.
2. Follow manufacturer's instructions to fuse paper-backed fusible web to wrong side of black check fabric (for birds), black fabric, and green fabric. Do **not** remove paper backing at this time.
3. To complete project, cut out the following:
   A — 2 (1 in reverse) from black check fabric
   G — 2 from gold fabric
   H — 2 (1 in reverse) from black fabric
   I — 4 (2 in reverse) from green fabric
   J — 4 from green fabric
4. To make patterns for collar and cuffs, trace around collar and cuffs. Add 1/2" to top edge of each pattern; cut out patterns. Use patterns to cut out 1 collar and 2 cuffs from black check fabric.
5. For bias binding, measure around outside edge of collar, each cuff, and each cape. Add 1" to each measurement. Using tan fabric for collar and cuffs, and black check fabric for cape, cut 3"w bias strips of fabric the determined measurements. Matching wrong sides and long edges, fold strips in half; press.

Assembling The Shirt

1. Remove paper backing from appliqués. Refer to photo for placement and follow manufacturer's instructions to fuse stems, leaves, birds, wings, and beaks to shirt. Use 3 strands of floss to **Blanket Stitch** (pg. 159) around appliqué pieces.
2. To make yo-yo flowers, turn raw edges under 1/4" and baste close to edge. Pull basting thread up to gather circle as tightly as possible; knot and clip ends of thread. Gathered side of flower is front.
3. Position each flower on shirt; place button in center of flower and sew flower to shirt through shank of button.

4. Remove buttons from cuffs. Press top edges of fabric collar and cuffs ½" to wrong side. Baste fabric collar and cuffs to right side of shirt collar and cuffs. Hand or machine sew pressed edges to shirt. Follow **Attaching Binding With Mitered Corners**, pg. 157, to attach binding to collar, cuffs, and cape edges using a ½" seam allowance and turning in raw edges ½" at beginning and end. Make new buttonholes in cuffs over old ones. Sew buttons to cuffs.

STUFFED BLACKBIRD

Size
Approximately 9" x 3"

Supplies
Black fabric — ⅜ yd of 45"w
2 black beads for eyes
2 black buttons for attaching wings
Polyester fiberfill
Dressmaker's tracing paper and tracing wheel

Instructions
1. Trace patterns **K-M**, pgs. 110-111, including all markings. Cut out patterns. Pin patterns to fabric; cut out fabric pieces.
2. To complete project, cut out the following:
   K — 2 (1 in reverse) from black fabric
   L — 1 from black fabric
   M — 4 (2 in reverse) from black fabric

Assembling The Blackbird
1. Use dressmaker's tracing paper and tracing wheel to transfer detail lines to right side of **K's** and **M's**.
2. For body, match right sides and sew **K's** together, leaving open between dots. Matching right sides, notches, and dots, sew **L** to body, leaving an opening for turning and stuffing. Clip curves; turn right side out. Stuff with fiberfill. Blind stitch opening closed.
3. Machine sew through all thicknesses along detail lines on tail.
4. For wings, match right sides and sew 2 **M's** together, leaving an opening for turning and stuffing. Clip curves; turn right side out. **Lightly** stuff with fiberfill. Blind stitch opening closed. Machine sew through all thicknesses along detail lines. Repeat to make remaining wing.
5. Refer to photo and pattern markings to position wings on body. Place buttons on wings and sew wings to body through button holes. Sew beads to body for eyes.

SUNFLOWER WALL HANGING

Size
28" x 40"

Supplies
Assorted tan fabrics — 1 yd of 45"w
Gold fabric — ⅓ yd of 45"w
Yellow fabric — ⅛ yd of 45"w
Brown fabric — ⅛ yd of 45"w
Blue fabric — 8" square
Stripe fabric for pants — ⅛ yd of 45"w
Black check fabric for fence — ⅛ yd of 45"w
Green fabric — 10" square
Scraps of black fabric for birds, hat, belt, and shoes
Assorted fabrics for border — total of ¼ yd of 45"w
Binding — ¾ yd of 45"w
Backing — 1 yd of 45"w
Fleece — 1 yd of 45"w
2 — ¼" buttons for eyes
14 assorted buttons
Six strand embroidery floss — black and green

Cutting Out Pieces
1. Follow **Making Templates**, pg. 147, to make templates from patterns **A**, **N-Q**, **S-U**, **FFF**, and **GGG** on pgs. 109-111. (*Note: Patterns for appliqué templates do not include seam allowance; add seam allowances to these pieces when they are cut out.*)
2. Follow **Cutting Out Quilt Pieces**, pg. 147, and cut out the following:
   A — 1 from black fabric
   N — 16 from gold fabric
   O — 16 from yellow fabric
   P — 3 from brown fabric
   Q — 8 from tan fabric
   R — 8 (3¾") squares from tan fabric
   S — 9 from black check fabric
   S — 9 from tan fabric
   T — 2 (1 in reverse) from black fabric
   U — 2 from green fabric
   V — 1 (3½" x 9½") piece from tan fabric
   W — 2 (1¾" x 4⅛") pieces from tan fabric
   X — 1 (1¾" x 2¼") piece from black fabric
   Y — 2 (1" x 3") pieces from tan fabric
   Z — 1 (1" x 4½") piece from black fabric
   AA — 2 (2½" x 4⅛") pieces from tan fabric
   BB — 1 (2½" x 2¼") piece from tan fabric
   CC — 2 (3¾" x 1¾") pieces from blue fabric
   DD — 1 (3" x 5½") piece from blue fabric
   EE — 2 (1¾" x 4¾") pieces from blue fabric
   FF — 2 (2½" x 4¾") pieces from tan fabric
   GG — 2 (1½" x 1") pieces from black fabric
   HH — 1 (1") square from gold fabric
   II — 2 (3¾" x 9") pieces from tan fabric
   JJ — 1 (3" x 3⅛") piece from stripe fabric
   KK — 2 (1½" x 6⅜") pieces from stripe fabric

LL — 1 (1" x 6³/₈") piece from tan fabric
MM— 2 (1³/₈" x 2¹/₂") pieces from tan fabric
NN — 2 (1³/₈" x 2³/₄") pieces from black fabric
OO — 1 (1" x 1³/₈") piece from tan fabric
PP — 1 (3" x 9¹/₂") piece from tan fabric
QQ — 1 (1¹/₄" x 9¹/₂") piece from green fabric
RR — 2 (2¹/₂" x 9¹/₂") pieces from tan fabric
SS — 1 (3³/₄" x 11¹/₂") piece from tan fabric
TT — 1 (2³/₄" x 11¹/₂") piece from tan fabric
UU — 1 (2¹/₂" x 6") piece from tan fabric
VV — 1 (5⁵/₈" x 6¹/₄") piece from tan fabric
WW — 1 (8³/₈" x 10") piece from tan fabric
XX — 4 (1¹/₂" x 9³/₄") pieces from black check fabric
YY — 3 (⁷/₈" x 10³/₄") pieces from tan fabric
ZZ — 1 (1¹/₂" x 7¹/₄") piece from tan fabric
AAA — 5 (1¹/₂" x 6¹/₄") pieces from black check fabric
BBB — 5 (⁷/₈" x 7¹/₄") pieces from tan fabric
CCC — 1 (7³/₄" x 13¹/₂") piece from tan fabric
DDD — 2 (1¹/₄" x 5⁵/₈") pieces from black check fabric
EEE — 2 (1¹/₄" x 8³/₈") pieces from black check fabric
FFF — 1 from gold fabric
GGG — 2 from gold fabric
HHH — 1 (4" x 24") piece from yellow fabric
Borders — 2 (3¹/₂" x 40¹/₄") lengths pieced from assorted fabrics

Assembling The Wall Hanging

1. To piece Sunflower block, follow **Piecing And Pressing**, pg. 148, and **Unit 1** diagram to sew pieces together to make **Unit 1**. Baste close to raw edge around center of **Unit 1**. Matching right sides, raw edges, and marks on **N's** to marks on **P**, pin **Unit 1** to **P**. Pull up basting thread, gathering **Unit 1** to fit **P**. Sew **P** to **Unit 1** to make **Unit 2**.

Unit 1   **Unit 2**

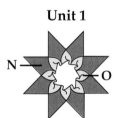   

2. Follow **Sewing Into A Corner**, pg. 150, and sew 4 **Q's** and 4 **R's** to **Unit 2** to complete **Sunflower Block**.

Sunflower Block

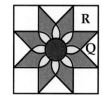

3. Repeat to make 2 **Sunflower Blocks**.
4. To piece fence blocks, sew 1 tan **S** to 1 black **S** to make **Unit 3**. Repeat to make 9 **Unit 3's**. Matching black triangles to **XX's**, sew 1 **Unit 3** to each **XX** to make 4 **Unit 4's**. Repeat to sew 1 **Unit 3** to each **AAA** to make 5 **Unit 5's**.

Unit 3   Unit 4   Unit 5

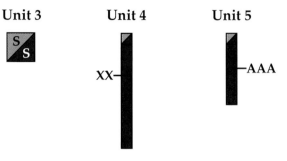

5. Sew 4 **Unit 4's** to 3 **YY's** to complete **Fence Block 1**. Sew 5 **Unit 5's** to 5 **BBB's**. Sew **ZZ** to **Unit 5** to complete **Fence Block 2**.

Fence Block 1   Fence Block 2

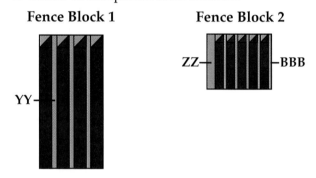

6. Follow **Assembly Diagram**, pg. 109, to assemble wall hanging top.
7. For borders, match right sides and raw edges and sew 1 (40¹/₄") border strip to each side of wall hanging top.
8. Refer to photo and **Quilting Diagram**, pg. 109, for placement, and follow **Hand Appliqué**, pg. 151, to appliqué **A**, **T's**, **U's**, and **DDD-GGG** to wall hanging top.
9. Use 3 strands of floss for all embroidery stitches. Refer to photo for placement and use black to **Outline Stitch** (pg. 159) birds' legs. Use green to **Outline Stitch** veins in leaves. Use black **Running Stitch** (pg. 145), for scarecrow's mouth.
10. For ruched flower, follow **Step 3** of **Appliquéd Jacket**, pg. 106, substituting **HHH** for **E**. Refer to **Quilting Diagram** for placement and sew flower to wall hanging top.
11. Appliqué remaining **P** to center of flower.
12. Follow **Marking Quilting Lines**, pg. 154, and **Quilting Diagram**, pg. 109, to mark quilting lines on wall hanging top.
13. Follow **Assembling The Quilt**, pg. 155, to layer backing, fleece, and wall hanging top and to baste all layers together.
14. Follow **Quilting**, pg. 156, and stitch wall hanging along marked lines. Trim batting and fleece even with edges of wall hanging.

15. Refer to photo for placement and sew buttons to wall hanging.
16. Follow **Making Continuous Bias Strip Binding**, pg. 156, and use a 27" square to make 4 yds of 2¹/₂"w bias binding.
17. Follow **Attaching Binding With Mitered Corners**, pg. 157, and attach bias binding to wall hanging.
18. Follow **Making A Hanging Sleeve**, pg. 158, to make and attach hanging sleeve to wall hanging.

Quilting Diagram

Assembly Diagram

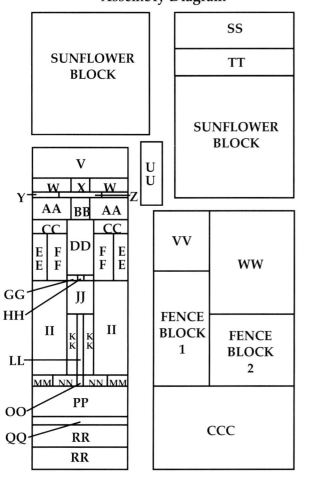

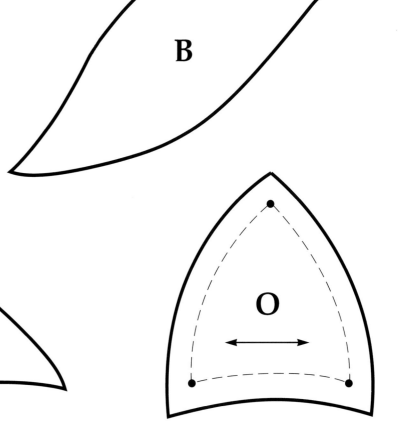

109

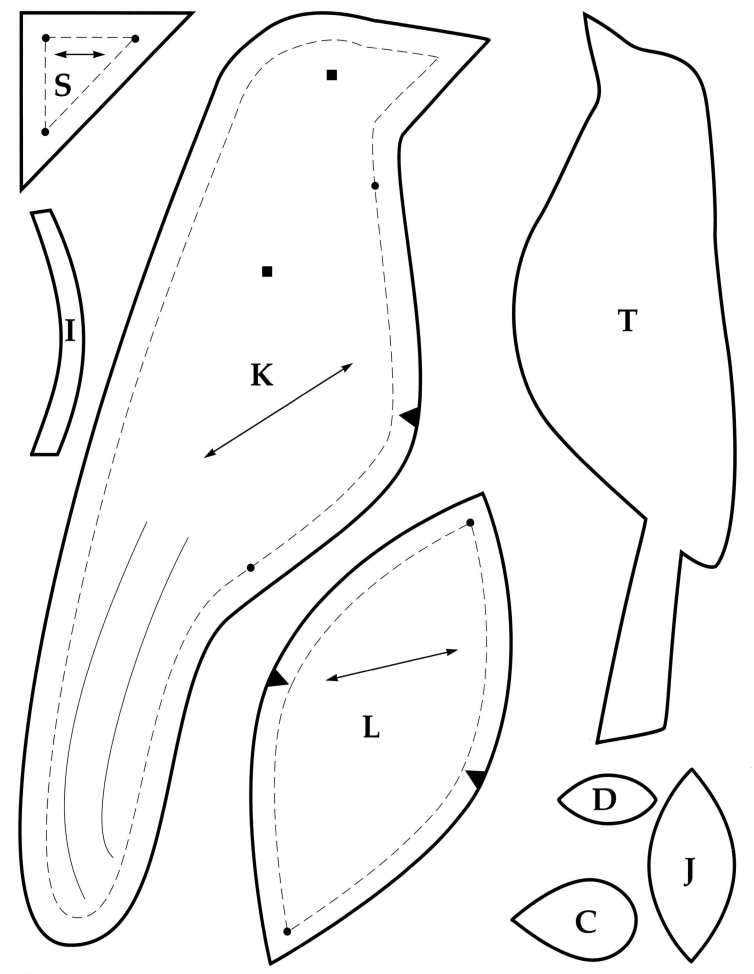

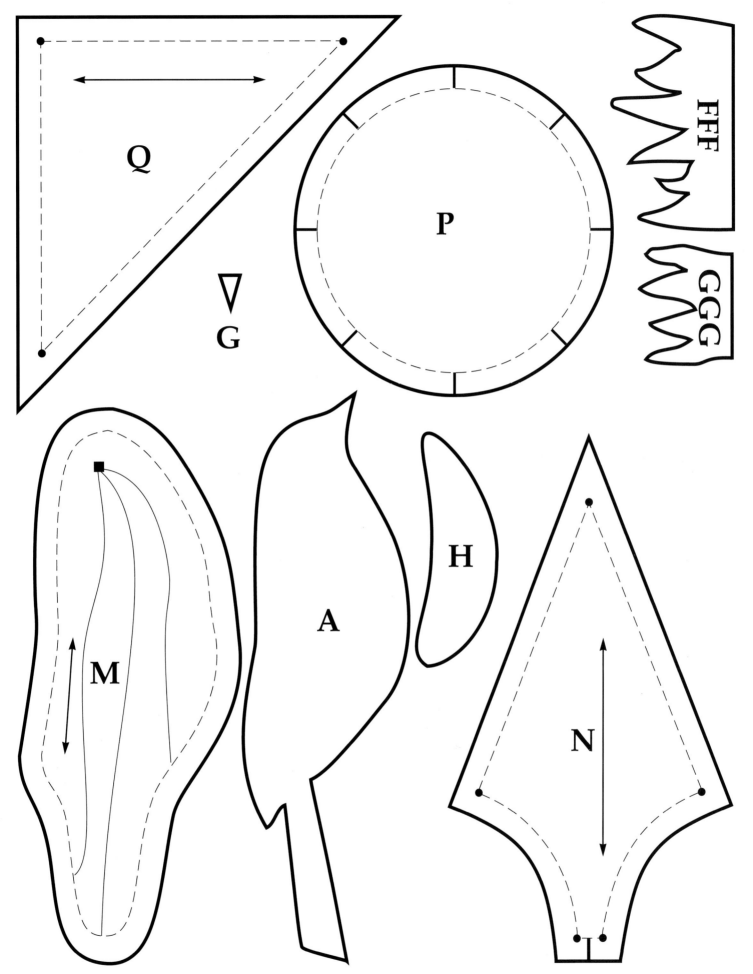

MARINER'S COMPASS

The Mariner's Compass pattern, a bold mixture of points and curves, dates from the early 1700's. Simulating the wind roses found on old compasses and sea charts, the dramatic design illustrates the close relationship of the American settlers to the sea. British ships laden with supplies frequently braved the rough Atlantic crossing, to be joyously greeted by colonists eager to hear news from home. Through the hard work of local fishermen, the sea also provided much of the food for the Colonial settlements. Reflecting the pioneering spirit of those early years, the quilt shown here is pieced in rich, masculine colors. Oak leaf appliqués and a Sawtooth sashing add to the striking beauty of the quilt.

MARINER'S COMPASS

Size

Block: 21" x 21"
Quilt: 93" x 109"

Yardage Requirements

Ecru fabric — 3 yds of 45"w
Tan fabric — 2½ yds of 45"w
Light blue fabric — ⅜ yd of 45"w
Medium blue fabric — 1⅞ yds of 45"w
Dark blue fabric for blocks and borders — 4½ yds of 45"w
Red fabric — 2¼ yds of 45"w
Binding — ½ yd of 45"w
Backing — 9¾ yds of 45"w **OR** 3¼ yds of 108"w
120" x 120" piece of low-loft polyester bonded batting

Cutting Out Pieces

1. Follow **Making Templates**, pg. 147, to make templates from all patterns on pgs. 116-119. *(Note: Patterns for appliqué templates **H** and **N** do not include seam allowances; add seam allowances to these pieces when they are cut out.)*

2. To complete our quilt you will need 6 whole blocks, 7 half blocks, and 2 quarter blocks. Follow **Cutting Out Quilt Pieces**, pg. 147, and cut out the following:
   Borders — 2 (11" x 88½") pieces from dark blue fabric
   Borders — 2 (11" x 93½") pieces from dark blue fabric
   A — 320 from ecru fabric
   B — 160 from medium blue fabric
   C — 80 from red fabric
   D — 71 from dark blue fabric
   E — 80 from light blue fabric
   F — 6 from dark blue fabric
   G — 31 from tan fabric
   ½ G (add ¼" seam allowance to grey line) — 9 from tan fabric
   ½ G (reversed) — 9 from tan fabric
   H — 31 from medium blue fabric
   ½ H — 9 from medium blue fabric
   ½ H (reversed) — 9 from medium blue fabric
   I — 9 from dark blue fabric
   I (reversed) — 9 from dark blue fabric
   J — 7 from dark blue fabric
   K — 2 from dark blue fabric
   L — 316 from ecru fabric
   L — 316 from red fabric
   L — 7 from medium blue fabric
   M — 40 from ecru fabric
   N — 40 from red fabric
   O — 2 from medium blue fabric
   P — 6 from medium blue fabric
   Binding — 2 (1½" x 94½") pieces
   Binding — 2 (1½" x 110") pieces

Assembling The Quilt

1. For each whole block, follow **Piecing And Pressing**, pg. 148, and **Sewing Together Pieces That Do Not Match Exactly**, pg. 150, and sew 1 **B** between 2 **A**'s to make **Unit 1**. Repeat to make a total of 16 **Unit 1's**. Sew 1 **C** between 2 **Unit 1's** to make **Unit 2**. Repeat to make a total of 8 **Unit 2's**. Sew 1 **E** to 1 **D** to make **Unit 3**. Repeat to make a total of 8 **Unit 3's**.

Unit 1

Unit 2

Unit 3

2. Follow **Unit 4** diagram and sew **Unit 2's** and **Unit 3's** together to make **Unit 4**. Follow **Sewing Curves**, pg. 150, and sew 1 **F** to **Unit 4** to make **Unit 5**.

Unit 4

Unit 5

3. Sew 4 **G's** together to make **Unit 6**.

Unit 6

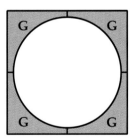

4. Sew **Unit 5** to **Unit 6**. Follow **Hand Appliqué**, pg. 151, and appliqué 1 **H** to each corner to complete **Whole Block**.

Whole Block

5. Repeat to make 6 **Whole Blocks**.
6. For each half block, follow **Half Block** diagram and sew pieces together in same order as **Whole Block**.

Half Block

7. Repeat to make 7 **Half Blocks**.
8. For each quarter block, follow **Quarter Block** diagram and sew pieces together in same order as **Whole Block**.

Quarter Block

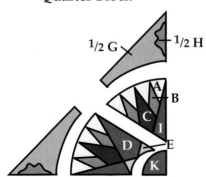

9. Repeat to make 2 **Quarter Blocks**.

10. For sashing, sew 8 ecru **L's** to 8 red **L's** to make **Unit 7**. Repeat to make a total of 20 **Unit 7's**.

Unit 7

11. Sew 1 **Unit 7** between 2 **M's** to make **Unit 8**. Hand appliqué 1 **N** to each end of **Unit 8**. Repeat to make a total of 20 **Unit 8's**.

Unit 8

12. Follow **Assembly Diagram** to sew **Blocks, Half Blocks, Quarter Blocks, Unit 8's**, and medium blue **L's, O's**, and **P's** together.

Assembly Diagram

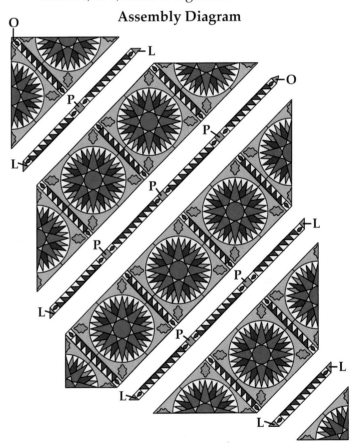

13. For top border, sew 34 ecru **L's** to 34 red **L's**. Repeat to make bottom border.
14. For side border, sew 44 ecru **L's** to 44 red **L's**. Repeat to make a total of 2 side borders.

15. Referring to **Quilt Top** diagram, sew borders to pieced blocks to complete **Quilt Top**.

Quilt Top

11" x 93¹/₂"

11" x 88¹/₂"

16. Follow **Marking Quilting Lines**, pg. 154, and **Quilting Diagram** and **Quilting Pattern**, pg. 117, to mark quilting lines on quilt top.

Quilting Diagram

17. Follow **Preparing Backing And Batting**, pg. 155, to piece backing if necessary.
18. Follow **Assembling The Quilt**, pg. 155, to layer backing, batting, and quilt top and to baste all layers together.

19. Follow **Quilting**, pg. 156, and stitch quilt along marked lines. Trim batting and backing even with edges of quilt.
20. Press one long edge of each binding piece ¹/₄" to wrong side. Matching right sides and raw edges and using a ¹/₄" seam allowance, sew 1 (110") piece of binding to each side of quilt. Trim short ends even with quilt. Fold binding over to quilt backing and pin pressed edge in place, covering stitching line. Blind stitch binding to backing.
21. With ends of binding extending ¹/₂" beyond quilt on each side, match right sides and raw edges and use a ¹/₄" seam allowance to sew 1 (94¹/₂") piece of binding each to top and bottom of quilt. Press short ends of binding ¹/₂" to wrong side. Fold binding over to quilt backing and pin pressed edge in place, covering stitching line. Blind stitch binding to backing.

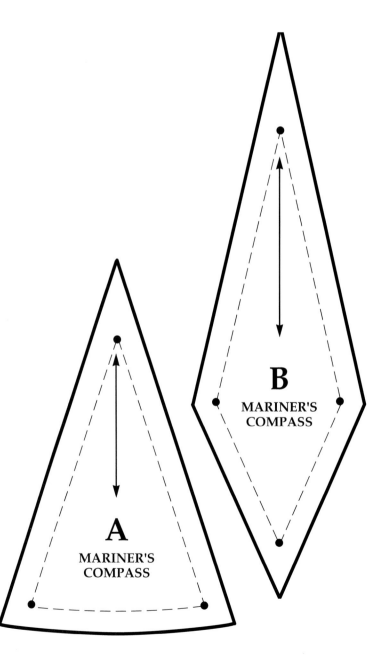

A
MARINER'S COMPASS

B
MARINER'S COMPASS

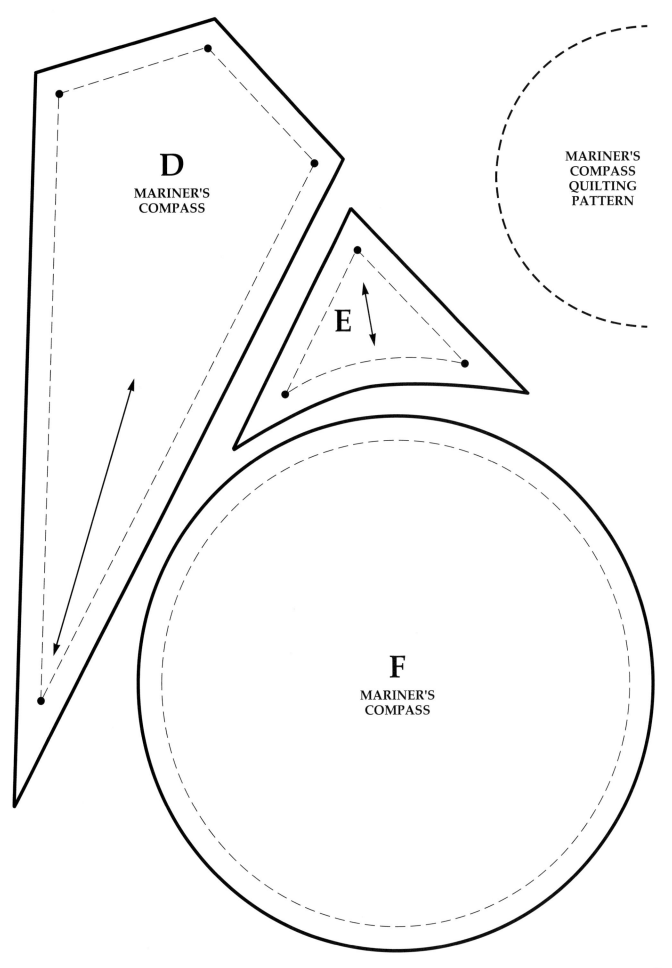

D
MARINER'S
COMPASS

E

MARINER'S
COMPASS
QUILTING
PATTERN

F
MARINER'S
COMPASS

117

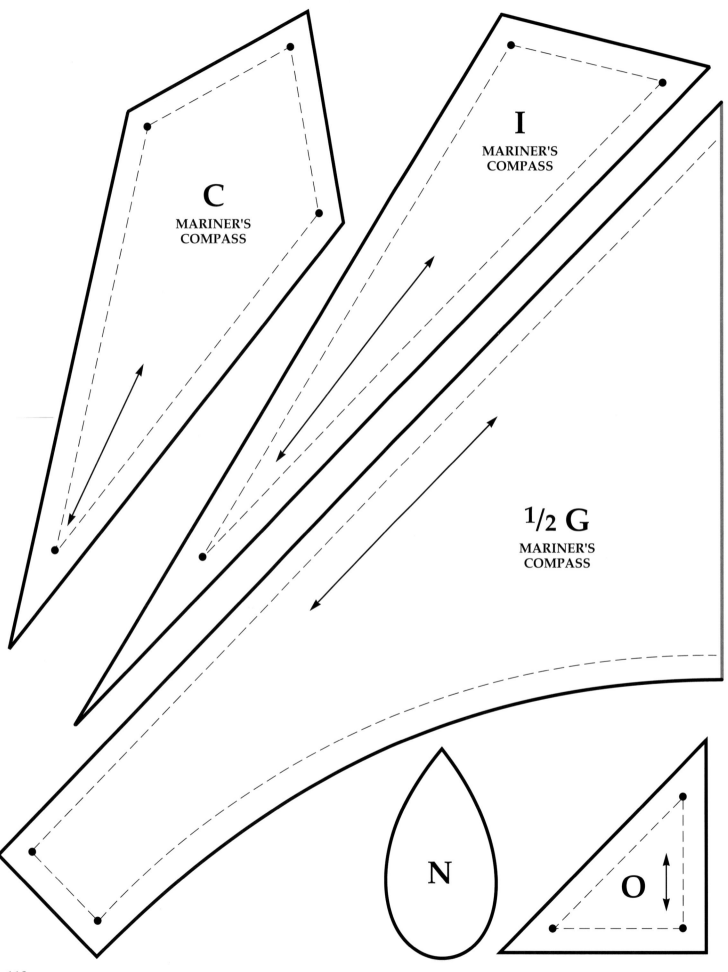

C
MARINER'S
COMPASS

I
MARINER'S
COMPASS

½ G
MARINER'S
COMPASS

N

O

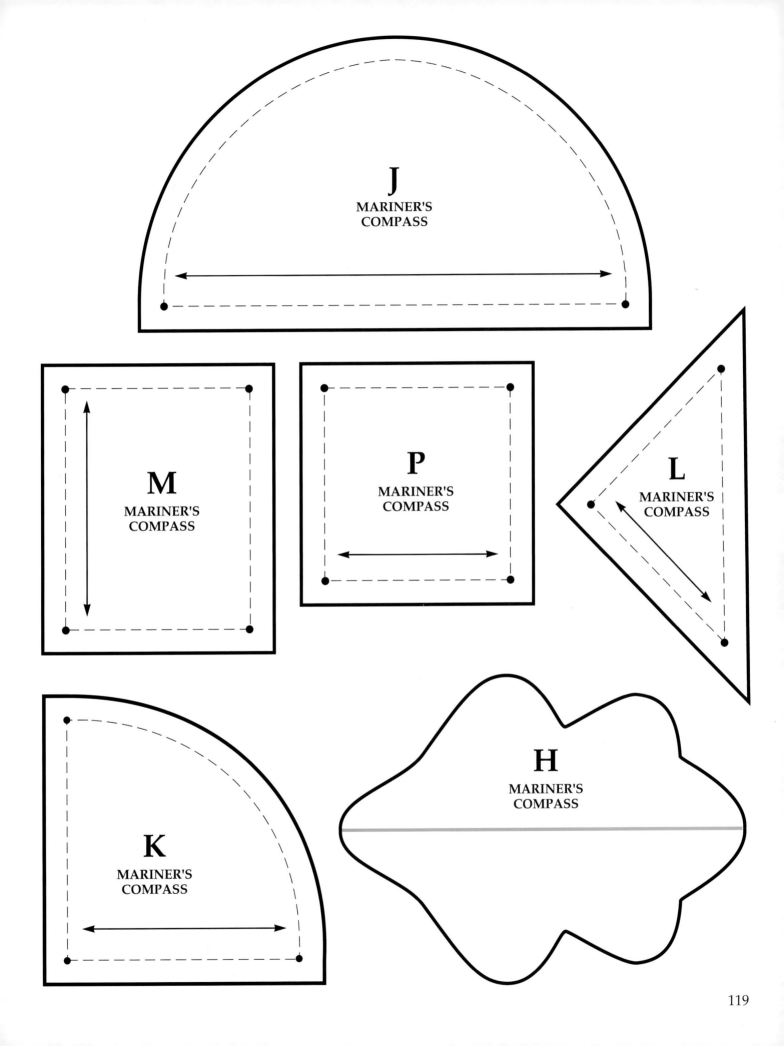

J
MARINER'S
COMPASS

M
MARINER'S
COMPASS

P
MARINER'S
COMPASS

L
MARINER'S
COMPASS

K
MARINER'S
COMPASS

H
MARINER'S
COMPASS

119

PINWHEEL QUILT

Swirling, twirling pinwheels have been favorite playthings for generations. And since so many traditional quilt patterns were inspired by scraps of the quilters' own lives, it's only natural that this colorful toy should show up in piecework. Quilters have created dozens of variations of the Pinwheel design over the years. Pieced with burgundy and navy fabrics combined with shades of brown and tan, this richly colored quilt is one of the simpler versions of the Pinwheel pattern. Each block contains four pieced pinwheels offset by strips of deep burgundy fabric. The use of the same burgundy fabric for the sashing, contrasted with navy corner blocks, gives the quilt a unified look.

PINWHEEL QUILT

Size
Block: 13" x 13"
Quilt: 75" x 91"

Yardage Requirements
Assorted light fabrics for pinwheels — total of 2 yds of 45"w

Assorted dark fabrics for pinwheels — total of 2 yds of 45"w

Dark red fabric for sashing and centers of blocks — 3¼ yds of 45"w

Blue fabric for setting squares — ¼ yd of 45"w

Binding — 1⅛ yds of 45"w blue fabric

Backing — 5½ yds of 45"w **OR** 2¾ yds of 90"w

81" x 96" piece of low-loft polyester bonded batting

Cutting Out Pieces
1. Follow **Making Templates**, pg. 147, to make templates from patterns **A** and **B**.
2. To complete our quilt you will need 30 blocks. Follow **Cutting Out Quilt Pieces**, pg. 147, and cut out the following:

    Sashing — 49 (13½" x 3") strips from dark red fabric

    Setting squares — 20 (3") squares from blue fabric

    A — 480 from assorted light fabrics

    A — 480 from assorted dark fabrics

    B — 60 from dark red fabric

    C — 30 (3" x 13½") pieces from dark red fabric

Assembling The Quilt
1. For each block, follow **Piecing And Pressing**, pg. 148, and sew 1 light fabric **A** to 1 dark fabric **A** to make **Unit 1**. Repeat to make a total of 16 **Unit 1's**. Sew 2 **Unit 1's** together to make **Unit 2**. Repeat to make a total of 8 **Unit 2's**.

Unit 1

Unit 2

2. Sew 2 **Unit 2's** together to make **Unit 3**. Repeat to make a total of 4 **Unit 3's**.

Unit 3

3. Sew 1 **B** between 2 **Unit 3's** to make **Unit 4**. Repeat to make a total of 2 **Unit 4's**.

Unit 4

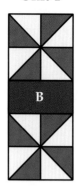

4. Sew 1 **C** between 2 **Unit 4's** to complete **Block**.

Block

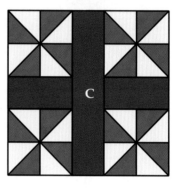

5. Repeat to make 30 **Blocks**.
6. Sew 4 sashing strips between 5 **Blocks** to make **Row 1**. Repeat to make **Rows 2-6**.

Row 1

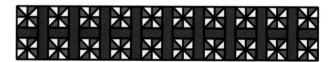

7. Sew 4 setting squares between 5 sashing strips to make **Unit 5**. Repeat to make a total of 5 **Unit 5's**.

Unit 5

8. Sew 1 **Unit 5** between **Row 1** and **Row 2**. Repeat to add **Rows 3-6** and remaining **Unit 5's** to complete **Quilt Top**.

Quilt Top

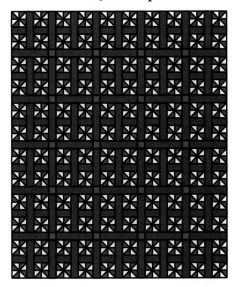

9. Follow **Marking Quilting Lines**, pg. 154, and **Quilting Diagram** to mark quilting lines on quilt top.

Quilting Diagram

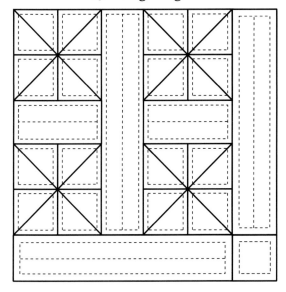

10. Follow **Preparing Backing and Batting**, pg. 155, to piece backing if necessary.
11. Follow **Assembling The Quilt**, pg. 155, to layer backing, batting, and quilt top and to baste all layers together.
12. Follow **Quilting**, pg. 156, and stitch quilt along marked lines. Trim batting and backing even with edges of quilt.
13. Follow **Making Continuous Bias Strip Binding**, pg. 156, and use a 36" square to make 10 yds of 2¹/₂"w bias binding.
14. Follow **Attaching Binding With Mitered Corners**, pg. 157, and attach bias binding to quilt.

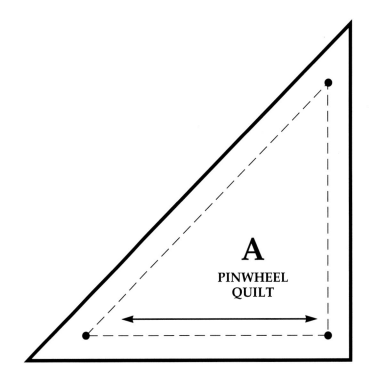

A
PINWHEEL QUILT

B
PINWHEEL QUILT

COZY CHRISTMAS

Frolicking snowmen abound in this fun-filled holiday collection! The frosty fellows appear on an appliquéd tree skirt and a wall hanging, and there's a cuddly stuffed figure, too. Other festive projects include pieced ornaments with tree and star motifs, and simple throw pillows. Shown here, a trio of snowmen gleefully juggles snowballs on the tree skirt, which features a plaid Prairie Point edging. These wintry accents are so cute you'll want to leave some out long past Christmas!

Snowmen sporting warm flannel scarves play beneath a star-studded sky on the appliquéd wall hanging. A colorful border of plaid fabrics adds cheer to the scene. Whether used alone or scattered among your favorite decorations, pieced patchwork ornaments lend a homey touch to the Christmas tree.

This jolly stuffed snowman makes a delightful holiday accent or gift! From his plaid earmuffs and scarf to his warm boots, he's dressed in wintry style. Decorative throw pillows sewn from festive checked fabrics turn any corner into a cozy hideaway.

TREE SKIRT

Size

46" diameter

Supplies

Blue fabric for background and bias binding —
2 yds of 45"w

3 assorted light fabrics for snow — ½ yd **each** of
45"w

White fabric for snowmen and snowballs — ⅜ yd
of 45"w

Black fabric for boots — 7" x 10" piece

Orange fabric for noses — 3" square

Assorted dark fabrics for hats, scarves, and
earmuffs — 6" square for **each**

Assorted gold fabrics for stars — 2 (6") and 4 (4")
squares

Dark fabric for prairie points — ¾ yd of 45"w

Fabric for backing — 1⅓ yds of 45"w

Fusible interfacing — 2¼ yds of 22"w

Paper-backed fusible web — 3 yds

Pellon® Stitch-N-Tear™ fabric stabilizer — 3 yds

3" — 6mm black chenille stem

5 — ⅝" white buttons

6 — ⅝" black buttons

4 — ¼" black buttons

Black six strand embroidery floss

Thread to coordinate with appliqués

Fleece — 1¼ yds of 45"w

Tracing paper

Instructions

1. Trace patterns **A-N** on pgs. 133-136. (Pattern **N**
is given as a ½ pattern. Fold tracing paper in
half and place fold along grey line of pattern;
trace black lines. Cut out along drawn lines.
Unfold pattern and press flat.)

2. Cut pieces of fusible interfacing slightly smaller
than all light-colored and white fabrics. Follow
manufacturer's instructions to fuse interfacing
to wrong side of fabrics.

3. Follow manufacturer's instructions to fuse
paper-backed fusible web to wrong side of light
fabric, white fabric, black fabric, orange fabric,
assorted dark fabric, and assorted gold fabric.
Do **not** remove paper backing at this time.

4. To complete project, cut out the following:
   Prairie Points — 33 (5") squares from dark
   fabric
   Binding — 1 (1½" x 60") bias strip from blue
   fabric (pieced if necessary)
   A — 5 from white fabric
   B — 3 from orange fabric
   C — 3 from white fabric for snowballs
   C — 2 from assorted dark fabric for earmuffs
   D — 3 from white fabric
   E — 6 (2 in reverse) from black fabric
   F — 1 from assorted dark fabric

G — 1 from assorted dark fabric
H — 1 from assorted dark fabric
I — 1 from assorted dark fabric
J — 1 from assorted dark fabric
K — 2 from assorted gold fabric
L — 2 from assorted gold fabric
M — 2 from assorted gold fabric
N — 10 from assorted light fabric

5. For tree skirt top, cut a 45" square of
background fabric. Fold fabric in half from top
to bottom and again from left to right; press. To
draw outer cutting line, tie one end of string to a
pencil near the tip. Insert thumbtack through
string 22" from pencil, then through folded
corner of fabric; draw one-fourth of a circle
(Fig. 1). To draw inner cutting line, repeat using
a 2¼" length of string between pencil and
thumbtack. Cutting through all thicknesses, cut
out tree skirt along drawn lines. Unfold fabric
once. Cut tree skirt opening by cutting along 1
fold line **(Fig. 2)**.

Fig. 1   **Fig. 2**

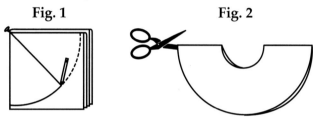

6. Use tree skirt top as a pattern to cut 1 backing
piece and 1 fleece piece.

Assembling The Tree Skirt

1. Place tree skirt top on ironing board. Remove
paper backing from appliqué pieces. Refer to
photo and **Placement Diagram** to position
appliqué pieces on tree skirt top, overlapping
pieces as necessary.

Placement Diagram

2. Follow manufacturer's instructions to fuse appliqué pieces to tree skirt top. Baste fabric stabilizer to wrong side of tree skirt top.

3. Follow **Machine Appliqué**, pg. 152, to appliqué design. Remove stabilizer; knot and trim thread ends.

4. Refer to photo for placement and use 3 strands of floss to **Outline Stitch** (pg. 159) snowmen's mouths.

5. Refer to photo for placement and sew buttons to snowmen. Sew chenille stem between earmuffs.

6. To make prairie points, fold one square in half from top to bottom; press. Fold side edges to meet long raw edges, forming a triangle *(Fig. 3)*; press. This will be the wrong side of the prairie point. Repeat with remaining squares.

Fig. 3

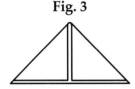

7. Matching right sides and raw edges, baste prairie points to right side of tree skirt top along outside edge.

8. *(**Note:** For all machine sewing, use a 1/4" seam allowance. Backstitch at beginning and ending of each seamline. Trim seam allowances to 1/8"; clip curves.)* Matching right sides and raw edges, place tree skirt backing on tree skirt top. Place fleece piece on wrong side of backing. Pin all layers together.

9. Machine sew through all layers along outside curved edge. Turn right side out; press. Baste raw edges together.

10. Matching wrong sides and long edges, fold binding in half. Follow **Attaching Binding With Mitered Corners**, pg. 157, to bind raw edges of tree skirt.

WALL HANGING

Size
34" x 29"

Supplies
Blue fabric for background — 1 yd of 45"w
Light fabric for snow — 1/4 yd of 45"w
White fabric for snowmen — 1/4 yd of 45"w
Black fabric for boots — 7" x 10" piece
Orange fabric for noses — 3" square
Assorted dark fabrics for hats, scarves, and earmuffs — 6" square for **each**
Assorted gold fabrics for stars — 1 (6") and 4 (4") squares
Gold fabric for inner border — 1/4 yd of 45"w
Assorted fabrics for border — total of 1/2 yd of 45"w
Fabric for backing — 1 yd of 45"w
Fabric for hanging sleeve — 3" x 32 1/4" piece
Fusible interfacing — 3/4 yd of 22"w
Paper-backed fusible web — 1 yd
Pellon® Stitch-N-Tear™ fabric stabilizer — 1 yd
3" — 6mm black chenille stem
5 — 5/8" white buttons
6 — 5/8" black buttons
4 — 1/4" black buttons
3 — 1" dia white pom-poms
Black six strand embroidery floss
Thread to coordinate with appliqués
Fleece — 1 yd of 45"w
Tracing paper

Instructions
1. Trace patterns **A-M** and **O** on pgs. 133-136. Cut out patterns. (Pattern **O** is given as a 1/2 pattern that is split into 2 pieces. Fold tracing paper in half and place fold along grey line of pattern **O**; trace black lines and ⊕'s. Place tracing paper on top of remaining half of pattern **O** matching ⊕'s and trace remainder of pattern. Cut out along drawn lines. Unfold pattern and press flat.)

2. Cut pieces of fusible interfacing slightly smaller than all light-colored and white fabrics. Follow manufacturer's instructions to fuse interfacing to wrong side of fabrics.

3. Follow manufacturer's instructions to fuse paper-backed fusible web to wrong side of light fabric, white fabric, black fabric, orange fabric, assorted dark fabric, and assorted gold fabric. Do **not** remove paper backing at this time.

4. To complete project, cut out the following:
   Background — 1 (27 1/4" x 22 1/4") piece from blue fabric
   Inner Borders — 2 (1 1/4" x 22 1/4") pieces and 2 (1 1/4" x 27 1/4") pieces from gold fabric
   Outer Borders — 2 (4" x 27 1/4") and 2 (4" x 29 1/4") border strips pieced from border fabrics
   Backing and Fleece —1 (29 1/4" x 34 1/4") piece from **each**
   A — 5 from white fabric
   B — 3 from orange fabric
   C — 2 from assorted dark fabric
   D — 3 from white fabric
   E — 6 (2 in reverse) from black fabric
   F — 1 from assorted dark fabric
   G — 1 from assorted dark fabric
   H — 1 from assorted dark fabric
   I — 1 from assorted dark fabric
   J — 1 from assorted dark fabric
   K — 2 from assorted gold fabric
   L — 2 from assorted gold fabric
   M — 1 from assorted gold fabric
   O — 1 from light fabric

Assembling The Wall Hanging

1. Place background fabric on ironing board. Remove paper backing from appliqué pieces. Refer to photo and **Placement Diagram** to position appliqué pieces on background fabric, overlapping pieces as necessary.

Placement Diagram

2. Follow manufacturer's instructions to fuse appliqué pieces to background. Baste fabric stabilizer to wrong side of background.
3. Follow **Machine Appliqué**, pg. 152, to appliqué design. Remove stabilizer; knot and trim thread ends.
4. Refer to photo for placement and use 3 strands of floss to **Outline Stitch** (pg. 159) snowmen's mouths.
5. Refer to photo for placement and sew buttons to snowmen and pom-poms to background. Sew chenille stem between earmuffs.
6. Matching wrong sides and long edges, fold inner border pieces in half; press.
7. (**Note:** *For all machine sewing, use a* $1/4$″ *seam allowance. Backstitch at beginning and ending of each seamline.*) Matching raw edges, sew 27$1/4$″ pieces of inner border to top and bottom of background; sew 22$1/4$″ pieces to sides of background.
8. Matching right sides and raw edges, sew 27$1/4$″ border strips to top and bottom edges of background; sew remaining border strips to sides.
9. Matching right sides and raw edges, place backing on wall hanging. Place fleece on wrong side of backing. Pin all layers together. Leaving an opening for turning, machine sew wall hanging to backing. Turn right side out; press. Blind stitch opening closed.
10. Follow **Making A Hanging Sleeve**, pg. 158, to make and attach hanging sleeve to wall hanging.

STAR ORNAMENT

Size
5″ x 5″

Supplies
Gold fabric — 6″ square
Blue fabric — 8″ square
Red fabric for backing — 7″ square
Fleece — 5″ square
$1/4$″w grosgrain ribbon — 8″

Cutting Out Pieces
1. Follow **Making Templates**, pg. 147, to make templates from patterns **P** and **Q** on pg. 136.
2. Follow **Cutting Out Quilt Pieces**, pg. 147, and cut out the following:
   P — 4 from gold fabric
   P — 4 from blue fabric
   Q — 1 from gold fabric
   Q — 4 from blue fabric
   R — 1 (6″) square for backing from red fabric

Assembling The Ornament
1. Follow **Block** diagram to sew pieces together to complete **Block**.

Block

2. Place backing wrong side up on a flat surface. Center fleece on wrong side of backing. Place block, right side up, on fleece. Pin block in place through all layers.
3. Fold each side edge of backing $1/4$″ to front; fold $1/4$″ to front again. Blind stitch folded edges in place. Repeat with top and bottom edges of backing. Fold ribbon in half and hand sew ends to back of ornament for hanger.
4. Machine sew around outside edges of star through all layers.

TREE ORNAMENT

Size
4¹⁄₂″ x 5¹⁄₂″

Supplies
Green fabric — 5″ square
Blue fabric — 4″ x 6″ piece
Black fabric — 2″ square
Red fabric for backing — 7″ x 8″ piece
Fleece — 4¹⁄₂″ x 5¹⁄₂″ piece
¹⁄₄″w grosgrain ribbon — 8″

Cutting Out Pieces
1. Follow **Making Templates**, pg. 147, to make templates from patterns **S-V** on pg. 136.
2. Follow **Cutting Out Quilt Pieces**, pg. 147, to cut out the following:
   S — 1 from green fabric
   T — 2 (1 in reverse) from blue fabric
   U — 2 from blue fabric
   V — 1 from black fabric
   W — 1 (5¹⁄₂″ x 6¹⁄₂″) piece from red fabric

Assembling The Ornament
1. Follow **Block** diagram and sew pieces together to complete **Block**.

Block

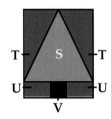

2. Follow **Steps 2-3** of **Star Ornament**, pg. 131, to back and bind ornament and to attach hanger.
3. Machine sew around outside edges of tree through all layers.

SNOWMAN

Size
Approximately 16″h

Supplies
White fabric for snowman — ¹⁄₂ yd of 45″w
Green fabric #1 for earmuffs — 7″ square
Green fabric #2 for scarf — ¹⁄₄ yd of 45″w
Orange fabric for nose — 3″ square
Gold fabric for star — 6″ x 12″ piece
Black fabric for boots — 10″ square
2 black shank-style buttons for eyes
2 black buttons for attaching boots
2 white buttons for attaching arms
9″ — 6mm black chenille stem
Black six strand embroidery floss
Paper-backed fusible web
Polyester fiberfill

4″ square of white poster board
Thick, clear-drying craft glue
Tracing paper

Instructions
1. For snowman body pattern, cut 1 (7″) circle and 1 (12¹⁄₂″) circle from tracing paper. Overlapping circles ³⁄₄″, tape circles together. Cut 2 snowman body pieces from white fabric.
2. Trace patterns **M** and **Y-BB** on pgs. 133 and 137. Cut out patterns.
3. Follow manufacturer's instructions to fuse paper-backed fusible web to wrong side of orange fabric and a 5″ x 10″ piece of green fabric #2. Do **not** remove paper backing at this time.
4. To complete project, cut out the following:
   M — 2 from gold fabric
   X — 1 (3¹⁄₂″ x 19¹⁄₂″) piece from green fabric #2
   Y — 1 from 5″ x 10″ green fabric #2
   Z — 4 (2 in reverse) from white fabric
   AA — 4 (2 in reverse) from black fabric
   BB — 1 from orange fabric

Assembling The Snowman
1. Remove paper backing from nose and scarf. Refer to photo for placement and follow manufacturer's instructions to fuse nose and scarf to right side of one snowman body.
2. Refer to photo for placement and use 3 strands of floss for all embroidery stitches. **Blanket Stitch** (pg. 159) around nose and scarf and **Outline Stitch** (pg. 159) mouth.
3. (***Note:*** *For all machine sewing, use a ¹⁄₄″ seam allowance. Backstitch at beginning and ending of each seamline. Clip curves and corners.)* Matching right sides and raw edges, pin and sew body pieces together, leaving bottom edge open for turning and stuffing. Turn body right side out; stuff with fiberfill. Blind stitch opening closed.
4. Repeat **Step 3** for arms, boots, and star.
5. Refer to photo for placement and position arms and boots on body. Place button on each arm and boot and sew to body through button.
6. For loose scarf piece, fringe ¹⁄₄″ of one short end of **X**. Press each long edge ¹⁄₂″ to wrong side. **Blanket Stitch** along each long edge of scarf.
7. Turn remaining short edge of scarf ¹⁄₄″ to wrong side. With scarf to back of body, sew end of scarf to shoulder at neck. Wrap scarf around neck; tack at shoulder over beginning end of scarf.
8. Refer to photo for placement and sew star to ends of each arm. Sew buttons to face for eyes.
9. For earmuffs, cut 2 (3″) circles and 2 (1³⁄₄″) circles of green fabric #1. Cut 2 (2″) circles of poster board.
10. Glue a small amount of fiberfill to one side of each poster board circle. Center each circle, fiberfill side down, on wrong side of 1 (3″) fabric circle. Fold and glue raw edges to back of circle.

11. Glue one end of chenille stem to back of each earmuff. Glue 1 remaining fabric circle to back of each earmuff.
12. Refer to photo for placement and sew earmuffs to head.

LARGE PILLOW

Size
17" x 17"

Supplies
Red fabric — 1/2 yd of 45"w
Green fabric — 1/2 yd of 45"w
Polyester fiberfill

Cutting Out Pieces
1. Cut 2 (17") squares of one fabric for pillow front and back.
2. Cut 1 (1 1/2" x 72") bias strip of remaining fabric (pieced if necessary).

Assembling The Pillow
(Note: For all machine sewing, use a 1/4" seam allowance.)
1. With **wrong** sides together, sew pillow backing to pillow top, leaving an opening at bottom edge. Stuff with fiberfill and sew final closure by hand or machine.
2. Matching wrong sides and long edges, fold binding in half. Follow **Attaching Binding With Mitered Corners**, pg. 157, to bind pillow.

SMALL PILLOW

Size
12 1/2" x 12 1/2"

Supplies
Border and backing fabric — 1/2 yd of 45"w
Red fabric — 7" x 13" piece
Green fabric — 7" x 13" piece
Polyester fiberfill

Cutting Out Pieces
1. To complete project, cut out the following:
   A — 2 (5 1/2") squares from red fabric
   A — 2 (5 1/2") squares from green fabric
   B — 2 (1 3/4" x 10 1/2") pieces from border fabric
   C — 2 (1 3/4" x 13") pieces from border fabric
   D — 1 (13") square from backing fabric

Assembling The Pillow
1. Follow **Piecing And Pressing**, pg. 148, to sew 2 green **A's** to 2 red **A's** to make **Unit 1**.

Unit 1

2. Sew 1 (10 1/2") border each to top and bottom of **Unit 1**. Sew 1 (13") border to each side of **Unit 1** to complete pillow top.
3. Follow **Step 11** of **Making Pillows**, pg. 158, to complete pillow.

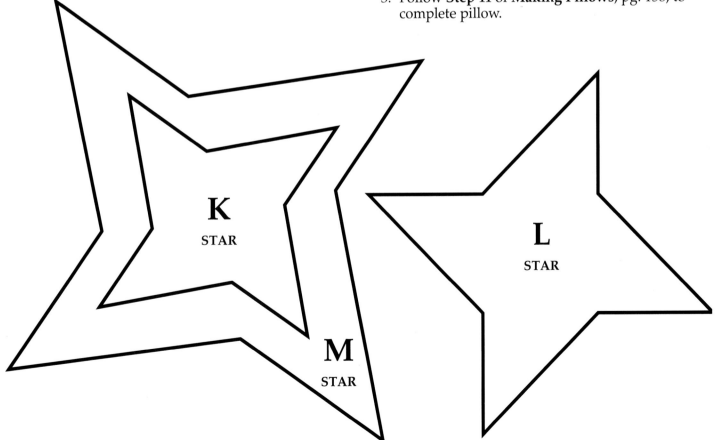

K
STAR

M
STAR

L
STAR

133

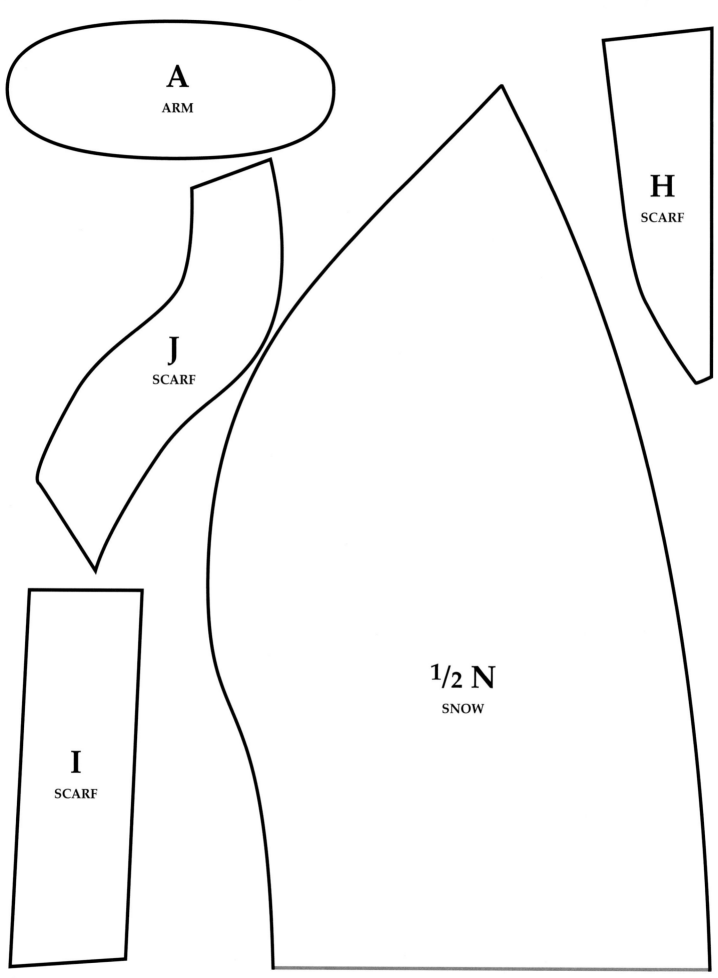

A
ARM

H
SCARF

J
SCARF

I
SCARF

½ N
SNOW

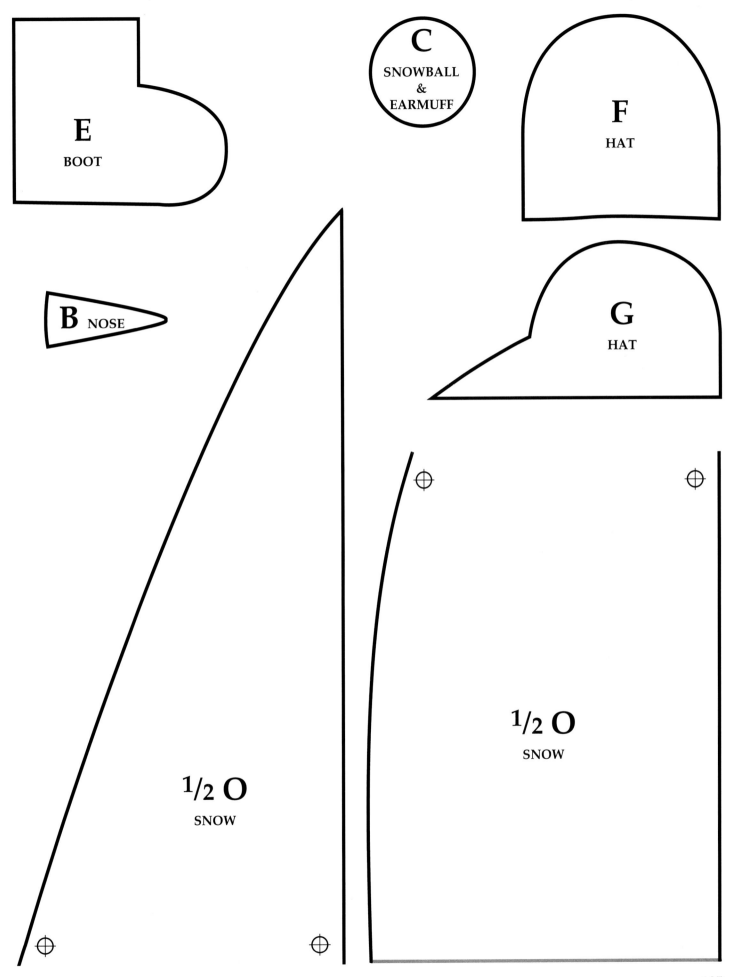

E
BOOT

C
SNOWBALL
&
EARMUFF

F
HAT

B NOSE

G
HAT

1/2 O
SNOW

1/2 O
SNOW

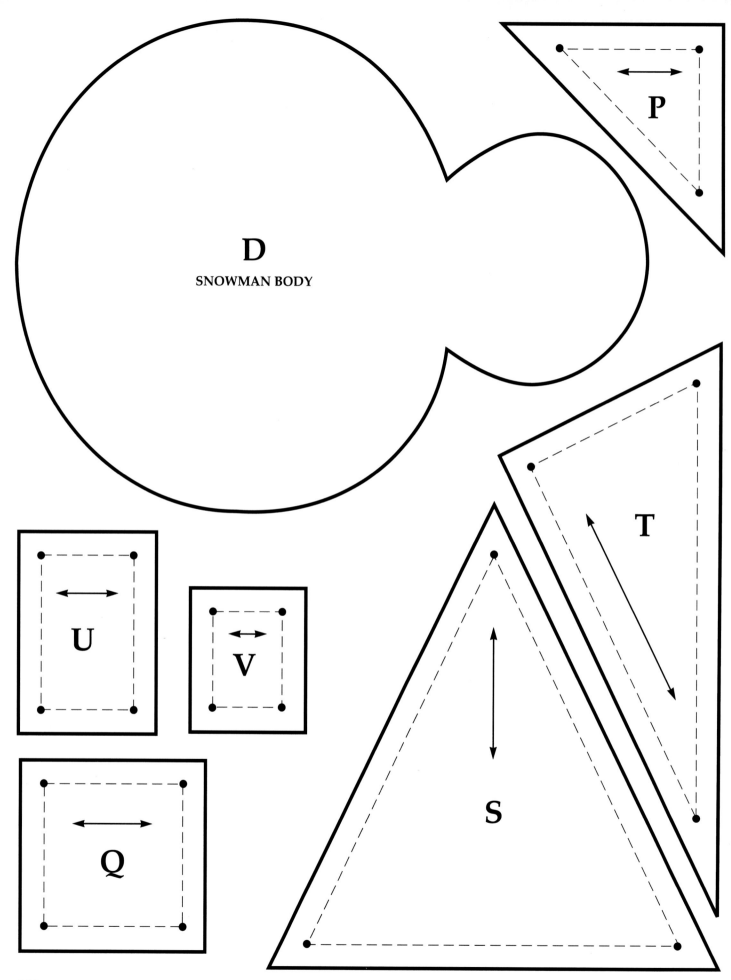

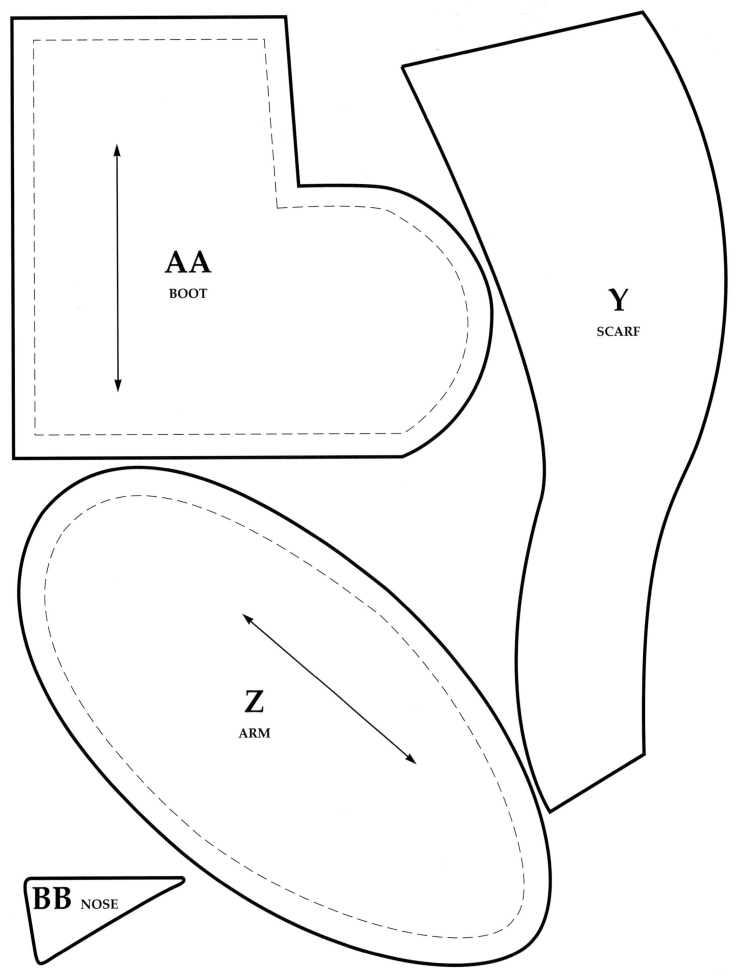

AA
BOOT

Y
SCARF

Z
ARM

BB NOSE

137

PRETTY PILLOWS

Crisp blue and white is a classic color scheme that's always been popular with quilters. To inspire you to sample a variety of the quilt patterns in our book, we created these patchwork pillows in a dreamy mixture of blues and white. These quick projects will make it easy and fun for you to try lots of different patterns. The Honey Bee design shown opposite is a charming combination of piecework and appliqué, with the rounded pieces representing the bee's wings and body. The pretty pillows pictured on the following pages feature patterns from other sections. By making the pillows in coordinating colors, such as we've done, you'll have a keepsake collection for grouping in a favorite room or corner of your home.

Decorative accents are reflections of who we are — especially in the needlewoman's home. These soft, comfortable throw pillows suggest warmth and hospitality. Perfect for dressing up a bed or piling in a chair, the lovely collection highlights quilt blocks from other sections of this book. The Bow Tie and Sawtooth pillows (opposite) are trimmed with pleasing ruffles. Created with deep indigo and Wedgwood-blue print fabrics, the Bear's Paw block is finished with a simple tailored look. Below, powder-blue pindots and twining leaves border the Churn Dash pillow, and the autographed Album block celebrates both quilting and the quilter.

ALBUM PILLOW

Size: 13″ x 13″

Supplies

White fabric — 6″ square
Light blue fabric (includes binding) — 3/8 yd of 45″w
Medium blue fabric (includes backing) — 1/2 yd of 45″w
Dark blue fabric — 12″ square
Muslin for pillow top backing — 15″ square
Fleece — 15″ square
Polyester fiberfill

Cutting Out Pieces

1. Follow **Making Templates**, pg. 147, to make templates from all patterns on pg. 101.
2. Follow **Cutting Out Quilt Pieces**, pg. 147, and cut out the following:
   A — 1 from white fabric
   A — 4 from dark blue fabric
   B — 2 from white fabric
   B — 8 from dark blue fabric
   C — 12 from medium blue fabric
   D — 4 from medium blue fabric
   E — 2 (2¹/₄″ x 10¹/₂″) pieces from light blue fabric
   F — 2 (2¹/₄″ x 14″) pieces from light blue fabric

Making The Pillow

1. Follow **Steps 1-5** of **Album Quilt**, pg. 100, to complete 1 block.
2. Follow **Steps 2-5** of **Making Pillows**, pg. 158, and **Quilting Diagram**, pg. 101, to complete pillow top and to cut pillow backing.
3. With **wrong** sides together, sew pillow backing to pillow top, leaving an opening at bottom edge. Stuff with polyester fiberfill and sew final closure by hand or machine.
4. For binding, cut a 2¹/₂″ x 60″ bias strip from light blue fabric (piece if necessary). Matching wrong sides and long edges, fold strip in half. Follow **Attaching Binding With Mitered Corners**, pg. 157, to bind pillow.

BEAR'S PAW PILLOW

Size: 12″ x 12″

Supplies

White fabric (includes backing) — 3/8 yd of 45″w
Medium blue fabric — 1/8 yd of 45″w
Dark blue fabric — 1/8 yd of 45″w
Muslin for pillow top backing — 14″ square
Fleece — 14″ square
Polyester fiberfill

Cutting Out Pieces

1. Follow **Making Templates**, pg. 147, to make templates from patterns **A-D** on pg. 95.
2. Follow **Cutting Out Quilt Pieces**, pg. 147, and cut out the following:
   A — 16 from dark blue fabric
   A — 16 from white fabric
   B — 4 from white fabric
   B — 1 from dark blue fabric
   C — 4 from medium blue fabric
   D — 4 from white fabric

Making The Pillow

1. Follow **Steps 1-5** of **Bear's Paw Quilt**, pg. 90, to complete 1 block.
2. Follow **Steps 2-5** and **Step 11** of **Making Pillows**, pg. 158, and **Quilting Diagram**, pg. 91, to complete pillow.

BOW TIE PILLOW

Size: 17″ x 17″ (including ruffle)

Supplies

White fabric (includes backing) — 3/8 yd of 45″w
Assorted blue fabrics — 3/8 yd of 45″w
Light blue fabric for ruffle — 1/2 yd of 45″w
Dark blue fabric (includes cording) — 1/2 yd of 45″w
Muslin for pillow top backing — 15″ square
Fleece — 15″ square
1/4″ dia cording — 1¹/₂ yds
Polyester fiberfill

Cutting Out Pieces

1. Follow **Making Templates**, pg. 147, to make templates from patterns **D** and **E** on pg. 59.
2. Follow **Cutting Out Quilt Pieces**, pg. 147, and cut out the following:
   D — 8 from white fabric
   D — 8 from assorted blue fabrics
   E — 4 from dark blue fabric

Making The Pillow

1. Follow **Step 1** of **Bow Tie Quilt**, pg. 58, to make 4 **Unit 2's**.
2. Follow **Block** diagram to sew **Unit 2's** together to complete **Block**.

Block

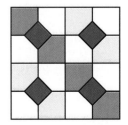

3. Follow **Steps 2-11** of **Making Pillows**, pg. 158, and **Quilting Diagram**, pg. 59, to complete pillow.

SAWTOOTH PILLOW

Size: 15" x 15" (including ruffle)

Supplies

White fabric (includes ruffle) — ½ yd of 45"w
Blue fabric (includes cording) — ½ yd of 45"w
Muslin for pillow top backing — 11" square
Fleece — 11" square
¼" dia cording — 1⅛ yds
Polyester fiberfill

Cutting Out Pieces

1. Follow **Making Templates**, pg. 147, to make template from pattern **A**.
2. Follow **Cutting Out Quilt Pieces**, pg. 147, and cut out the following:
   A — 24 from white fabric
   A — 24 from blue fabric
   B — 4 (1½" x 3½") pieces from blue fabric
   C — 1 (3½") square from blue fabric
   C — 4 (3½") squares from white fabric

Making The Pillow

1. Follow **Steps 1-3** of **Sawtooth Quilt**, pg. 17, to make 1 block.
2. Follow **Steps 2-11** of **Making Pillows**, pg. 158, and **Quilting Diagram**, pg. 19, to complete pillow.

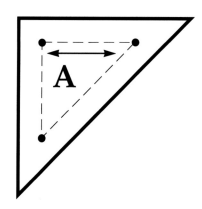

CHURN DASH PILLOW

Size: 17" x 17"

Supplies

White fabric — ⅛ yd of 45"w
Light blue fabric — ¼ yd of 45"w
Medium blue fabric (includes backing) — ½ yd of 45"w
Muslin for pillow top backing — 19" square
Fleece — 19" square
Polyester fiberfill

Cutting Out Pieces

1. Follow **Making Templates**, pg. 147, to make templates from patterns **A** and **B** on pg. 69.
2. Follow **Cutting Out Quilt Pieces**, pg. 147, and cut out the following:
   A — 4 from white fabric
   A — 4 from medium blue fabric
   B — 5 from white fabric
   B — 4 from medium blue fabric
   C — 4 (4½" x 9¼") pieces from light blue fabric
   D — 4 (4½") squares from medium blue fabric

Making The Pillow

1. Follow **Steps 1-3** of **Churn Dash Quilt**, pg. 65, to complete 1 block.
2. Follow **Block** diagram to sew **C's** and **D's** to block.

Block

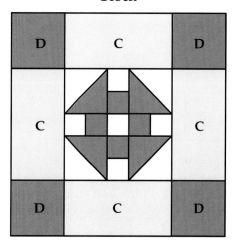

3. Follow **Steps 2-5** and **Step 11** of **Making Pillows**, pg. 158, and **Quilting Diagram**, to complete pillow.

Quilting Diagram

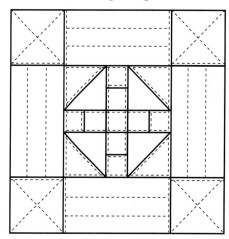

HONEY BEE PILLOW

Size: 12" x 12"

Supplies
White fabric — 10" square
Light blue fabric (includes backing) — 3/8 yd of
 45"w
Medium blue fabric — 1/8 yd of 45"w
Dark blue fabric (includes binding) — 1/2 yd of
 45"w
Muslin for pillow top backing — 14" square
Fleece — 14" square
Polyester fiberfill

Cutting Out Pieces
1. Follow **Making Templates**, pg. 147, to make
 template from pattern **D**. *(**Note:** Pattern for
 appliqué template **D** does not include seam
 allowance; add seam allowance when pieces are cut
 out.)*
2. Follow **Cutting Out Quilt Pieces**, pg. 147, and
 cut out the following:
 A — 5 (2¹/₂") squares from white fabric
 A — 4 (2¹/₂") squares from medium blue fabric
 B — 4 (3¹/₂" x 6¹/₂") pieces from light blue fabric
 C — 4 (3¹/₂") squares from medium blue fabric
 D — 12 from dark blue fabric

Making The Pillow
1. Sew 5 white **A's** to 4 blue **A's** to make **Unit 1**.

Unit 1

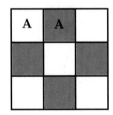

2. Follow **Block** diagram and sew **B's** and **C's** to
 Unit 1. Follow **Hand Appliqué**, pg. 151, and
 appliqué **D's** to **Block**.

Block

3. Follow **Steps 2-5** of **Making Pillows**, pg. 158,
 and **Quilting Diagram** to complete pillow top
 and to cut pillow backing.

Quilting Diagram

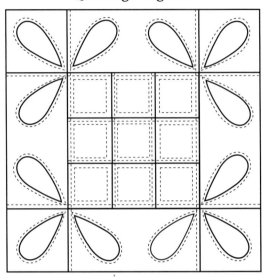

4. With **wrong** sides together, sew pillow backing
 to pillow top, leaving an opening at bottom
 edge. Stuff with fiberfill and sew final closure by
 hand or machine.
5. For binding, cut a 2¹/₂" x 54" bias strip from
 dark blue fabric (piece if necessary). Matching
 wrong sides and long edges, fold strip in half.
 Follow **Attaching Binding With Mitered
 Corners**, pg. 157, to bind pillow.

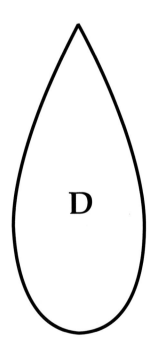

GENERAL INSTRUCTIONS

QUILTING TERMS

Appliqué — A cutout piece of fabric that is sewn to a larger background piece of fabric.

Backing — The back or bottom layer of a quilt.

Backstitch — A reinforcing stitch taken at the beginning and end of a seam to secure stitches. To backstitch by hand, bring needle up through fabric at 1, go down at 2, and come up at 3 *(Fig. 1)*. To backstitch by machine, reverse stitching and stitch on top of previously sewn stitches *(Fig. 2)*.

Fig. 1	**Fig. 2**

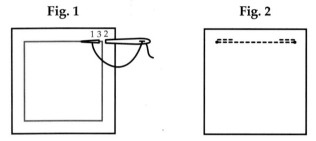

Basting — Large Running Stitches *(Fig. 4)* used to temporarily secure pieces or layers of fabric together. After securing layers with permanent stitches, remove basting stitches.

Batting — The middle layer of a quilt; provides the insulation and warmth as well as the thickness.

Bias — The diagonal direction on a piece of fabric in relation to the crosswise and lengthwise grains *(Fig. 3)*. Quilt pieces cut on the bias will stretch and distort easily.

Binding — May refer to the enclosing or covering of the raw edges of a quilt. May also refer to the fabric strip used to bind the edges.

Border — Strips of fabric that are used to frame a quilt top.

Grain — The direction of threads woven in the fabric. "Crosswise grain" refers to the threads running from selvage to selvage. "Lengthwise grain" refers to the threads running parallel to the selvages *(Fig. 3)*.

Fig. 3

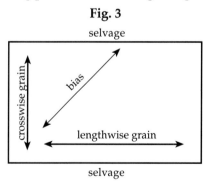

Mitered corner — Refers to a method used to finish corners of quilt border or binding.

Piecing — Sewing the pieces of a quilt design together to form a quilt block or an entire quilt top.

Piecing Stitch — A Running Stitch in which each series of stitches begins with a Backstitch.

Quilt block — Fabric pieces sewn together to make one unit of a quilt. Blocks are sewn together to form a quilt top.

Quilt top — The decorative part of a quilt that is layered on top of the batting and backing.

Quilting — May refer to the actual stitching together of the three quilt layers: top, batting, and backing. May also refer to the entire process of making a quilt.

Running Stitch — A series of straight stitches with the stitch length equal to the space between stitches. Take needle in and out of fabric several times before completely pulling needle and thread through fabric *(Fig. 4)*.

Fig. 4

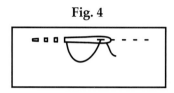

Sashing — Strips of fabric in a quilt top that separate the individual quilt blocks.

Selvages — The two finished lengthwise edges of the fabric *(Fig. 3)*. Selvages should be trimmed from fabric before cutting out pieces, as the tightly woven fibers could cause pieces to pucker.

Straight grain — The crosswise or lengthwise grain of fabric *(Fig. 3)*. Quilt pieces cut on lengthwise grain are least likely to stretch. Quilt pieces cut on crosswise grain will stretch only a very small amount. Each pattern is marked with an arrow, which should be lined up with straight grain.

Template — A pattern that is made from a durable material, such as posterboard, manila folders, or clear plastic sheets.

QUILTING SUPPLIES

There are many things to consider when purchasing your quilting supplies. If you are a beginning quilter, you may not wish to invest a large amount of money in supplies, but buy the best quality products you can afford.

Appliqué needle — These needles, sometimes called "sharps," are thinner than other sewing needles and are used for appliqué, basting, and hand piecing. A size 10 or 12 sharp works well.

Batting — The middle layer of a quilt. Batting is most commonly available in polyester, cotton, or a blend of polyester and cotton. We recommend that beginners choose a low-loft polyester bonded batting. A low-loft batting is thinner or flatter than a high-loft batting and is easier to quilt through. When batting is bonded, it has gone through a process to prevent the fibers from separating and coming through the fabric.

Clear plastic sheets — May be used for making templates. Clear plastic templates are durable, remain accurate after many uses, and can easily be placed on the fabric along straight grain or along design of fabric.

Cutting mat — A special mat designed to be used with a rotary cutter.

Eraser — A soft white fabric eraser or white art eraser may be used to remove pencil marks. Do not use a colored eraser; the dye may discolor fabric.

Fabric — Used for quilt top, backing, and binding. Types of fabrics to choose are found under **Selecting Fabrics**.

Freezer paper — Used for making cardboard templates and for stabilizing fabric for signing and dating the quilt.

Iron — Used for pressing prewashed fabrics before cutting out quilt pieces and for pressing seam allowances.

Lightweight cardboard — May be used for making templates. White posterboard or manila folders are good choices.

Marking tools — Used to draw around templates on fabric and to mark placement lines and quilting lines on quilt top.

Permanent fine point marker — Used to mark clear plastic sheets when making templates and to sign and date quilts. Test marker to make sure it will not bleed on fabric or wash out.

Quilt soap — Mild soap designed to remove dirt, oils, and finishes from fabrics without the use of chemicals that may shorten the life of the quilt.

Quilting hoop — Designed to securely hold the three layers of a quilt while you quilt. An embroidery hoop is designed to hold only one layer of fabric and is not considered a substitute for a quilting hoop. We recommend that you quilt with a 14" or 18" hoop. A larger size will make it difficult to reach the center with the hand that is underneath the quilt. Also, quilting with a hoop of this size instead of using a large frame allows you to quilt in your lap and makes your quilting portable.

Quilting needle — These needles, called "betweens," come in numbered sizes such as 8, 9, 10, and 12. The higher the number the shorter the needle. Betweens are shorter and thinner than regular sewing needles, allowing you to work through layered fabric easier and to make smaller stitches. We recommend that beginning quilters use a size 8 or 9 needle. More advanced quilters may wish to use a size 10 or 12 needle in order to achieve smaller stitches.

Quilting thread — This thread is stronger than regular sewing thread and has a coating that makes it slide easily through the quilt layers. Cotton-covered polyester quilting thread is strong and readily available. At first, you may wish to choose a neutral color so that variations in the size of stitches will not be obvious.

Rotary cutter — A cutting tool made up of a round, sharp blade mounted on a handle. May be used to cut fabric. A rotary cutter is especially helpful in cutting long strips of fabric, such as sashing and border strips. Should be used with a cutting mat and ruler.

Ruler — Used when marking straight lines on templates and on fabric. A clear plastic ruler with 1/8" measurements marked crosswise and lengthwise aids in accurate markings. An 18" quilter's ruler has such markings and is commonly used. An Omnigrid® ruler, which is thicker and made of harder plastic than a quilter's ruler (but also has 1/8" markings), also works well, especially when using a rotary cutter.

Scissors — A pair of sharp scissors is needed for cutting fabric. A separate pair of scissors for cutting out templates is recommended. Fabric-cutting scissors should not be used for cutting out templates because the blades will soon become dull and make cutting fabric difficult. You may also wish to keep a small pair of scissors handy for clipping threads.

Seam ripper — Used for ripping out stitching that must be removed.

Sequin pins or trim pins — These pins are shorter than regular straight pins and are easier to work around when appliquéing. Available in 1/2" and 3/4" lengths; the 3/4" may be easier to handle.

Sewing machine — May be used for piecing quilt blocks, assembling quilt top, attaching binding, and making pillows.

Sewing thread — Used for basting, piecing, and appliquéing. Cotton or cotton-covered polyester thread is strong and readily available. If you are working with all dark fabrics, use a dark thread. If you are working with all light fabrics, use a light thread. Most often in quilting, you will be working with a variety of colors and shades; in this case, use a neutral color, such as ecru or grey.

Straight pins — Used to secure fabric pieces for sewing. Pins should be sharp and clean so that they will slide in and out of the fabric easily.

Thimble — Used when sewing and quilting to protect the finger that pushes the needle through the fabric. Thimbles are available in metal, plastic, and leather, and in many sizes. Using a thimble may seem awkward at first, but with practice you will not want to work without one.

1/4" wheel — Sometimes called Quilter's Wheel. May be used to draw the cutting line when preparing to cut out quilt pieces for hand piecing.

SELECTING FABRICS

100% cotton fabrics are best for quilting. Choose a good-quality, tightly woven fabric that is not sheer. 100% cotton fabrics hold a crease better, fray less, and are easier to quilt than cotton blends. Check end of fabric bolt for fabric content and width.

The colors you choose for your quilt are very important. Color is seen first, even before design and workmanship. Light colors emphasize an area of a quilt, while dark colors cause an area to recede. The colors you choose should have contrast to make them a little more exciting to the eye. If you are not sure that two fabrics have enough contrast, take a small piece of each to a copy machine and make a black and white copy of them. This allows you to see the contrast without being confused by the colors. Above all, when selecting your color scheme, make sure the colors are pleasing to you. If a fabric matches or blends, but is not a fabric you really like, change it. You will be much happier with the quilt in the long run.

A mixture of solids and prints is pleasing to the eye. You may wish to use all solids or all prints. If you choose all prints, be sure to vary the size and type of the prints to add interest and contrast. For example, you may try flowers, dots, and hearts.

If you wish to use a directional fabric, such as a stripe or plaid, consider its position in the quilt and take care when cutting out pieces. Stripes and plaids are the most obvious directional fabrics, but you should also take care when working with a small design printed in rows. Buy an additional 1/2 yd if using directional fabric. This enables you to line up arrows on templates with the design of the fabric if it is printed off grain, rather than following the straight grain of the fabric. The design of the fabric overrides the grain. Handle these pieces carefully, as you may be working with bias edges which stretch easily.

PREPARING FABRICS

All fabrics should be washed, dried, and pressed before you begin work on your quilt. Even if you do not plan to wash your quilt in the future, it is important to wash the fabric before you begin. Washing removes sizing, preshrinks fabric, and checks for color fastness. Washing also makes the fabric easier to quilt through and will remove chemicals that may shorten the life of your quilt.

Dark colors such as red, blue, green, or black may bleed when washed. To check these colors, fill a sink about half full with very warm water. Place one end of fabric in water and agitate with your hands. Gently squeeze water from fabric. If water is not clear, wash fabric separately until rinse water runs clear. If fabric continues to bleed, choose another fabric.

To prevent the fabric from raveling when being washed, snip a small triangular piece from each corner of the fabric.

To wash fabrics, separate fabrics by color and machine wash in warm water using a small amount of quilt soap (made for quilts and fine fabrics), or a small amount of mild laundry detergent if quilt soap is not available. Do not use fabric softener. Rinse fabric at least three times to make sure all finishes are removed from fabric. Dry fabrics in the dryer, checking long fabric lengths occasionally to make sure that they are not tangling. To make ironing easier, remove fabrics from dryer while they are slightly damp.

MAKING TEMPLATES

Making templates is a very important step in quilt making. If your templates are inaccurate, you will find it impossible to piece quilt blocks together correctly. Use a ruler when drawing straight lines for templates. Place finished template over pattern to check for accuracy.

If a half pattern is given, fold tracing paper in half and place folded edge along grey line on pattern. Carefully trace pattern, including all markings. Turn traced pattern over and trace all markings to other half of pattern. Open traced pattern; press flat and make template.

If a quarter pattern is given, fold tracing paper in half and in half again. Place folded edges along grey lines on pattern. Carefully trace pattern, including all markings. Turn traced pattern over and trace all markings to other quarter of pattern. Open one fold and trace remainder of pattern. Open traced pattern; press flat and make template.

Patterns for the piecing templates in this book have two lines: a sewing line (dashed line) and a cutting line (solid line). **The cutting line is traced for machine piecing**; a 1/4" seam allowance is included. **The sewing line is traced for hand piecing**; you will add the 1/4" seam allowance to these pieces when they are cut out. Patterns for appliqué templates have only one line — the sewing line. These patterns do not include a seam allowance; you will add the seam allowance to these pieces when they are cut out.

FROM CLEAR PLASTIC SHEETS
For clear plastic templates, place plastic sheet on pattern. Using a permanent fine point marker, trace dashed line for hand piecing or solid line for machine piecing. Trace arrow for straight grain. Write pattern letter and name of block on template. Carefully cut out template along traced lines.

FROM LIGHTWEIGHT CARDBOARD
For cardboard templates, lay freezer paper shiny side down on pattern. Use #2 pencil or permanent marker to trace dashed line for hand piecing or solid line for machine piecing. Trace arrow for straight grain. Do not cut out pattern at this time. Place freezer paper shiny side down on cardboard. With iron set at "Cotton" setting (without steam), place iron on freezer paper for 3-5 seconds. Cut out template. Write pattern letter and name of block on template.

CUTTING OUT QUILT PIECES

Before cutting any fabric, follow **Preparing Fabrics**, to wash, dry, and press all fabrics to be used in the quilt.

CUTTING SASHING AND BORDERS
To make sure you have enough fabric for long borders and sashing strips, cut them first, before cutting out quilt pieces. These strips are cut along the lengthwise grain of the fabric to keep them from stretching and to eliminate the need to piece strips. Take care to cut strips the exact widths given. To be cautious, you may wish to cut the strips longer than needed and trim to required length. Because it is easy to confuse the strips after they are cut, pin a piece of paper on each strip on which you have written the measurements of the strip. Strips may be cut traditionally, using scissors, or they may be cut using a rotary cutter. Read the following sections thoroughly and follow either method to cut strips.

TRADITIONAL METHOD
The traditional method involves measuring and marking with a ruler and marking tool, then cutting with scissors. Use a ruler to mark a straight line along lengthwise grain next to selvage; cut selvage from fabric. Mark and cut desired width strips for sashing and borders.

ROTARY CUTTER METHOD

Place cutting mat on a flat surface. Lay fabric on cutting mat with one raw edge in front of you and one selvage on the left *(Fig. 5)*. Place ruler on edge of fabric, aligning one of the vertical lines over the selvage. Place the blade of the cutter against the edge of the ruler. Beginning with the cutter near you and rolling the blade **away** from you, roll blade on the mat before you reach the fabric. Keeping the blade against the edge of the ruler, roll the blade away from you while holding ruler down firmly with other hand. Move next section of fabric onto mat and repeat to trim selvage from desired length of fabric.

Fig. 5

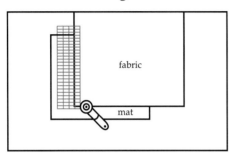

Beginning with trimmed edge of fabric on the left, place ruler on fabric with the measurement for the width of the strip on the trimmed edge of fabric. For example, to cut 3" wide sashing strips, place the 3" vertical marked line of the ruler on the trimmed edge of fabric and use rotary cutter as described above to cut strip. If your ruler is narrower than the strips you are going to cut, measure and mark width of strip on fabric; then line up edge of ruler with markings and roll cutter along edge of ruler to cut strips.

FOR MACHINE PIECING

Lay template on **wrong** side of fabric, lining up arrow with straight grain. This will help keep the fabric from stretching. *(Note: If your fabric has a directional pattern, such as a stripe or plaid, line up arrow on template with design of fabric, even if it is not on straight grain.)*

With marking tool at an angle (to prevent skipping) and with tip against edge of template, carefully draw around template. Since templates contain seam allowances, there is no need to leave space between quilt pieces. Line up edge of template with line of previously drawn piece and draw around template. The pieces will share a cutting line.

It is important to transfer the dots that are at the corners of patterns to fabric; these will help you sew set-in seams and align pieces that do not match exactly, such as a triangle being sewn to a square.

FOR HAND PIECING

Lay template on **wrong** side of fabric, lining up arrow with straight grain *(Note: If your fabric has a directional pattern, such as a stripe or plaid, line up arrow on template with design of fabric, even if it is not on straight grain.)*

With marking tool at an angle (to prevent skipping) and with tip against edge of template, carefully draw around template. This is your sewing line. Leaving at least ¹/2" between drawn shapes to allow for seam allowances, repeat for required number of quilt pieces. Cut out each quilt piece approximately ¹/4" outside drawn line. Disregard the dots that are at the corners of patterns. These dots are for use in machine piecing and are not necessary for hand piecing; this is because hand piecing involves sewing only from one end of a sewing line to the other and not sewing into seam allowances.

SPECIAL SITUATION

Some quilt pieces are to be cut out with the template reversed. For reversed pieces, simply turn template over before drawing around template.

PIECING AND PRESSING

Accuracy is very important when piecing. To help you remember the placement of the pieces, lay out pieces as they will appear when the block is completed. Then, following individual instructions for piecing order, pick pieces up as you need them, sew them together, and lay them back down with other pieces.

When piecing some blocks, ends of seam allowances will extend past edges of pieces; trim ends of seam allowances even with edges of pieces.

MACHINE PIECING

Set sewing machine for approximately eleven stitches per inch. Use a needle suited for medium weight fabric and make sure the needle is sharp. For many sewing machines, the measurement from the needle to the outer edge of the presser foot is ¹/4". If this is the case with your machine, you may use the presser foot as a guide to sew a ¹/4" seam allowance. If not, measure ¹/4" from the needle and mark the seam allowance on the sewing machine with a piece of masking tape. Or, use a ruler and marking tool to mark sewing lines ¹/4" from raw edges on wrong side of each quilt piece.

Use regular sewing thread (not quilting thread) to piece by machine. Stitch on scrap fabric first to check upper thread and bobbin thread tension and make any adjustments necessary to the machine before you begin to piece.

Any time you are using straight pins while piecing, remove the pins as they get close to the sewing machine needle. Do not sew over pins, as it may cause the needle to move or break, or may even jam the machine.

To begin piecing, place pieces right sides together and match raw edges; pin pieces together. For pieces that do not match exactly, insert a pin through dot at one corner of each piece; repeat at corner on opposite end of seamline *(Fig. 6)*; pin pieces together.

Fig. 6

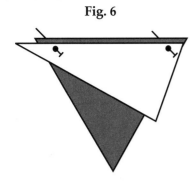

In most cases while machine piecing, you will sew from one edge of the fabric to the other, sewing into the seam allowances. However, when you will be sewing into a corner you will only sew between the dots, backstitching at beginning and end of sewing line *(Fig. 7)*. This will allow you to pivot the piece in order to sew the next seam precisely. *(**Note:** When sewing from one edge of fabric to the other, it is not necessary to backstitch at beginning and end of stitching. Stitches will be secured by intersecting seams.)*

Fig. 7

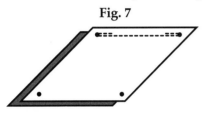

HAND PIECING

To begin piecing, thread a sewing needle with a single length of sewing thread; make a small knot in one end. Place pieces right sides together, carefully matching drawn lines. Insert a pin through one end of drawn line on both pieces; repeat at opposite end of drawn line *(Fig. 8)*; pin pieces together.

Fig. 8

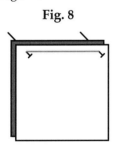

Take a backstitch at one end of drawn line. Using a Piecing Stitch (approximately 7-10 stitches per inch), stitch pieces together along drawn line, checking both

sides of fabric as you sew to make sure your stitches are straight, even, and directly on drawn line. With practice, your stitches will also be small. Do not sew into or across seam allowance; backstitch at end of drawn line *(Fig. 9)*. Knot and clip thread.

Fig. 9

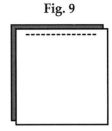

PRESSING

Planning your pressing is very important. The following guidelines will help you decide which way, and when to press seam allowances. In machine piecing, press seam allowances as you sew. In hand piecing, press when you complete a section or a block rather than pressing each seam as you sew. In hand or machine piecing, seam allowances are almost always pressed to one side, not open; this gives strength to the seam. The seam allowances are generally pressed toward the darker fabric. However, to reduce bulk in certain areas, it may be necessary to press the seam allowances toward the lighter fabric or even press them open.

When you are matching seams to sew rows together, seam allowances must face opposite directions. Also, seam allowances from strips should be pressed in one direction to distribute bulk. Pieces that radiate out from the center should also be pressed in one direction, either clockwise or counterclockwise.

To help distribute bulk after sewing through seam intersections, it is necessary to press seam allowances open at the intersection. In hand piecing, use your finger to open seam allowances at the intersection; press *(Fig. 10)*. In machine piecing, you will need to use a seam ripper to remove stitches in the seam allowance past the intersection; then press seam allowances open. This does not weaken the seams; they are still secured where the stitching lines cross.

Fig. 10

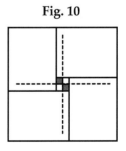

In order to eliminate shadowing, which is a dark fabric seam allowance showing through a light fabric, trim the darker seam allowance slightly narrower than the lighter seam allowance.

SEWING THROUGH INTERSECTIONS

To sew through intersections by machine, place pieces right sides together and match seams, making sure seam allowances are facing opposite directions. To prevent fabric from shifting, pin seam allowances in place.

To sew through intersections by hand, place pieces right sides together, match seams, and pin. Sew pieces together along drawn line until you reach the intersection. Take a backstitch and insert needle through intersection *(Fig. 11)*. Backstitch on other side of intersection and continue to sew as before.

Fig. 11

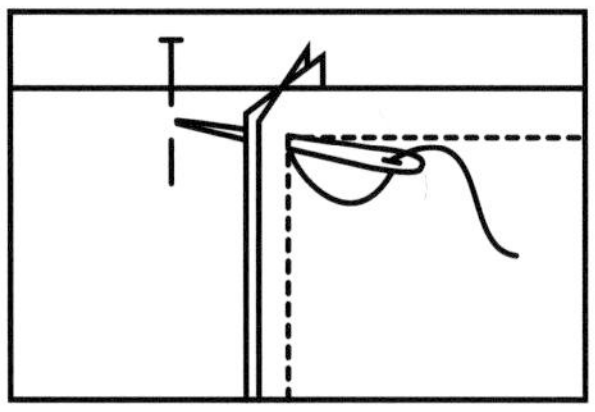

SEWING TOGETHER TRIANGLES WITH BIAS EDGES

Because bias edges stretch, be careful not to stretch fabric when sewing pieces with bias edges together. After sewing the seam, carefully press seam allowances to one side, again making sure you do not stretch the fabric. These precautions will help all pieces in the block fit together precisely.

SEWING TOGETHER PIECES THAT DO NOT MATCH EXACTLY

(Note: If machine piecing, it is important to transfer dots to your templates and to fabric pieces. These are important when sewing together pieces with edges that do not match exactly. If hand piecing, continue to mark and follow sewing line as usual.) Place pieces right sides together, carefully matching dots *(Fig. 12)*; pin pieces together. Sew from fabric edge to fabric edge, not just between the dots, when joining these pieces.

Fig. 12

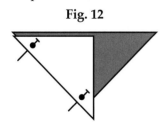

SEWING CURVES

It is important that you mark center of edges on curved pieces, as indicated on patterns. Place pieces right sides together, matching centers *(Fig. 13)*. Pin curved edges together at center and corners, clipping as needed *(Fig. 14)*. Pin edges together between center and corners, easing in fullness as shown in **Fig. 15**. Sew pieces together along the curved seamline. *(Note: In hand piecing, make sure you match and sew through the drawn line on both pieces.)*

Fig. 13

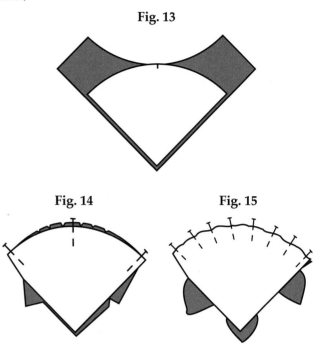

Fig. 14   **Fig. 15**

SEWING INTO A CORNER OR SETTING IN SEAMS

When piecing blocks such as Bow Tie, there are times when the piece you add will have two or more adjoining edges to sew to the pieces you have already sewn. This is called sewing into a corner, or setting in seams. To do so, you will sew the seam on one edge of the added piece, then pivot the piece and sew the next seam.

Matching right sides, pin the new piece to the piece on the left. Stitch seam from the outer edge to the dot at the inside corner *(Fig. 16)*.

Fig. 16

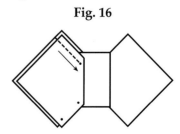

Pivot the added piece to sew the second seam. Pin and sew as before, beginning with the needle in the hole of the last stitch taken and ending at the second dot *(Fig. 17)*.

Fig. 17

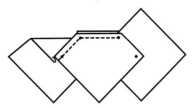

Pivot the added piece again and sew as before, beginning with the needle in the hole of the last stitch taken *(Fig. 18)*.

Fig. 18

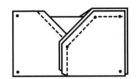

HAND APPLIQUÉ

APPLIQUÉ METHOD

The **Simple Basting** method involves basting the seam allowance of the appliqué in place before the appliqué is positioned on the background fabric.

1. Place template on right side of appliqué fabric.
2. Use marking tool to draw around template. Leaving at least 1/2″ between shapes, repeat for number of shapes specified. Cut out each shape approximately 3/16″ outside drawn line. Clip inward points up to, but not through, drawn line *(Fig. 19)*.

Fig. 19

3. Thread appliqué needle with a single strand of sewing thread; knot one end.

4. For each appliqué shape, begin on as straight an edge as possible and turn a small section of seam allowance to wrong side with your fingers, concealing the drawn line. Use a Running Stitch to baste seam allowance in place *(Fig. 20)*. (**Note:** *Do not turn seam allowances under that will be covered by other appliqué pieces.*)

Fig. 20

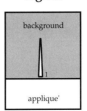

5. Continue basting around shape. When basting curves, work a small area at a time; you may even need to take one stitch at a time on curves to gently ease in fullness.
6. When all shapes have been basted, pin shapes to background fabric.
7. Use **Appliqué Stitch** to appliqué shapes to fabric. Remove basting thread and pins from each appliqué shape.
8. Follow **Cutting Away Fabric From Behind Appliqués** to reduce bulk behind appliqués.

APPLIQUÉ STITCH

The **Appliqué Stitch** is an invisible stitch used to secure a folded edge of fabric to a background fabric. Match color of thread to color of appliqué; this will help disguise your stitches. Thread appliqué needle with a 20-24″ length of sewing thread; knot one end. Stitches should be approximately 1/16″ apart, and never longer than 1/8″. Bring needle up through background fabric at 1 *(Fig. 21)*; needle should come up even with edge of appliqué. Insert needle in folded edge of appliqué at 2, directly across from 1; bring needle out of folded edge at 3 *(Fig. 22)*. Insert needle into background fabric at 4, even with edge of appliqué and directly across from 3; bring needle back up through background fabric at 5 *(Fig. 23)*, forming a small stitch on wrong side of fabric. Stitches on right side of fabric should not show. Stitches in folded edge of appliqué and on background fabric should be equal in length. Repeat stitches as shown in **Figs. 22** and **23** until you have completely secured edge of appliqué in place. Secure and clip thread.

Fig. 21	**Fig. 22**	**Fig. 23**

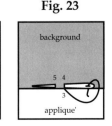

PRESSING APPLIQUÉD BLOCKS

To keep from distorting appliqués when pressing blocks with appliquéd shapes, place towel on ironing board and place the block face down on the towel. Press block from wrong side.

CUTTING AWAY FABRIC BEHIND APPLIQUÉS

Quilting an appliquéd block will be easier if you are stitching through as few layers as possible. For this reason, or just to reduce bulk in your quilt, you may want to cut away the background fabric behind the appliqués. After stitching the appliqués in place, turn the block over. Use sharp scissors to trim away the background fabric to approximately $3/16"$ from stitching line *(Fig. 24)*; take care not to cut appliqué fabric or any stitches.

Fig. 24

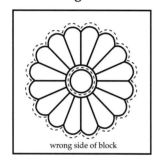

wrong side of block

MACHINE APPLIQUÉ

A satin stitch, also known as an appliqué stitch, is a thick, almost solid line of stitching used to cover raw edges of appliqué designs. A smooth satin stitch is important to the appearance and durability of the finished design. Practice is essential for obtaining an even stitch with good coverage, especially on corners and curves. Stitching corners and curves at a slow speed is helpful.

1. Set sewing machine for a medium width zigzag stitch ($1/16"$ to $1/8"$ wide) and a short stitch length (18-24 stitches per inch). Set upper tension slightly looser than for regular stitching. Refer to your sewing machine manual, if necessary, to make these adjustments.
2. (**Note:** *All designs with layered appliqué pieces are to be stitched beginning with the pieces that are at the bottom of the layers and ending with the pieces that are on the top.*) Beginning on as straight an edge as possible, position fabric under presser foot so that most of the satin stitch will be on the appliqué piece. At starting point of stitching, do not backstitch; hold upper thread toward you and sew over it 2-3 stitches. (This will keep thread from raveling.) Following **Steps 3-6** for stitching corners and curves, stitch over all exposed raw edges of appliqué pieces and along detail lines. Do not backstitch at end of stitching. All threads will be pulled to wrong side of background fabric and secured when stitching is completed.

3. (**Note:** *Dots on **Figs. 25-30** indicate where to leave needle in fabric when pivoting.*) For **outside corners**, stitch $1/16"$ to $1/8"$ (the width of your satin stitch) past the corner, stopping with the needle in **background** fabric *(Fig. 25)*. Raise presser foot. Pivot project, lower presser foot, and stitch adjacent side *(Fig. 26)*.

Fig. 25   **Fig. 26**

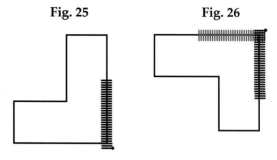

4. For **inside corners**, stitch $1/16"$ to $1/8"$ (the width of your satin stitch) past the corner, stopping with the needle in the **appliqué** fabric *(Fig. 27)*. Raise presser foot. Pivot project, lower presser foot, and stitch adjacent side *(Fig. 28)*.

Fig. 27   **Fig. 28**

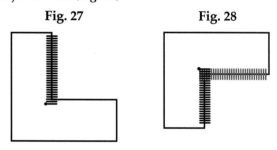

5. On **slight** curves, pivoting is not necessary; turn project slightly as needed while stitching. On **extreme outside** curves, stop with needle in **background** fabric. Raise presser foot and pivot project; the amount to pivot depends on the severity of the curve. Lower presser foot and continue stitching, pivoting as often as necessary to follow curve *(Fig. 29)*.

Fig. 29

6. On **extreme inside curves**, stop with needle in the **appliqué** fabric. Raise presser foot and pivot project; the amount to pivot depends on the severity of the curve. Lower presser foot and continue stitching, pivoting as often as necessary to follow curve *(Fig. 30)*.

Fig. 30

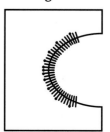

ADDING MITERED BORDERS

Seam allowances are included in border measurements. (**Note:** *If hand piecing, mark a 1/4" seam allowance on each edge.*) The border lengths include several extra inches for "insurance;" do not trim extra length until corners have been mitered. When sewing, match right sides and raw edges and use a 1/4" seam allowance.

1. Matching short edges, fold top border strip in half; mark center of raw edge. Pin center of border strip to top center of quilt top. From center of border strip, measure out 1/2 the width of the quilt top in both directions and mark. Match marks on border strip with corners of quilt top and pin. Easing in any fullness, pin border strip to quilt top between center and corners.
2. Sew border strip to quilt top beginning and ending **exactly** 1/4" from each corner of quilt top, backstitching at beginning and end of stitching line (*Fig. 31*). Do **not** sew into seam allowance.

Fig. 31

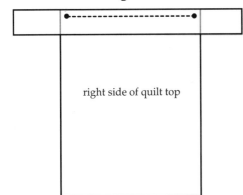

3. Repeat **Steps 1** and **2** to sew another border strip to bottom edge of quilt top.
4. To temporarily move top and bottom border strips out of the way, fold ends of strips and pin as shown in **Fig. 32**.

Fig. 32

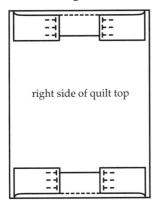

5. Follow **Step 1** to pin remaining border strips to sides of quilt top.

6. Sew one side border strip to quilt top beginning and ending **exactly** 1/4" from each corner of quilt top, backstitching at beginning and end of stitching line (*Fig. 33*). (*Note: Stitching should begin and end exactly at ends of previous stitching lines.*) Do not sew into seam allowances. Repeat to sew remaining border strip to quilt top.

Fig. 33

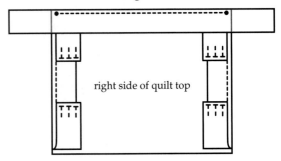

7. Press seam allowances toward border strips.
8. Lay quilt top right side down on a flat surface. Overlap top and bottom border strips over side border strips.
9. Mark underneath strip on outer edge at the point where strips overlap (*Fig. 34*).

Fig. 34

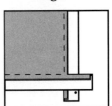

10. Matching right sides and raw edges, bring strips together with marked strip on top. Use ruler to draw a line from the mark on the outer edge of strip to the end of the stitching line (*Fig. 35*). Pin strips together along drawn line. Sew directly on drawn line, backstitching at beginning and end of stitching (*Fig. 36*).

Fig. 35   **Fig. 36**

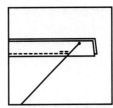   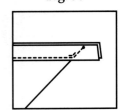

11. Turn mitered corner right side up. Check to see that there is not a gap at the inner end of the seam and that corner does not pucker. If necessary, use seam ripper to remove seam; carefully pin and sew seam again.
12. Trim seam allowances to 1/4". Press seam allowances to one side.
13. Repeat **Steps 8-12** to miter each remaining corner.

MARKING QUILTING LINES

MARKING TOOLS

There has been much discussion recently about the different kinds of marking tools available to the quilter. Fabric marking pens have been available for a relatively short time, and we do not yet know their long term effects on fabric. Still, many quilters use them and are very happy with the results. If you choose a fabric marking pen, be sure to follow the manufacturer's instructions for removing the marks.

Lead pencils, silver colored pencils, and white fabric marking pencils are also very popular with quilters. Keep any pencil sharp to ensure the accuracy of the quilt block, as thick lines will add width to quilt pieces. A mechanical pencil is very helpful as the lead is always sharp, allowing you to make a thin, clear line. Lead pencils work well on light-colored fabric and silver or white pencils work well on dark-colored fabric. Press down with pencil only as hard as is needed to make a visible line. Marks need to remain on the fabric until you are through quilting, and should be easy to remove. Most markings are removed when the fabric is washed.

To choose marking tools, **test** different markers **on scrap fabric first** until you find the ones that give the desired results. If marks are not easily removed from the fabric, try another marking tool.

TYPES OF QUILTING

IN THE DITCH

Quilting close to the edge of a seam (*Fig. 37*) or appliqué (*Fig. 38*) is called "In The Ditch." This type of quilting does not need to be marked. When quilting In The Ditch, quilt on the side **opposite** the seam allowance.

Fig. 37

Fig. 38

OUTLINE

Quilting approximately 1/4" from a seam or appliqué is called "Outline" quilting. This type of quilting is indicated on diagrams by dashed lines a short distance from solid lines. This type of quilting may be marked to ensure an accurate quilting line. It is easiest to mark these lines before basting quilt layers together. Use a ruler to mark straight lines. Or, place 1/4"w masking tape on the quilt to mark straight lines; then quilt directly beside the edge of tape. (*Note: Do not leave the tape on the quilt any longer than is necessary. Remove the tape when you are through quilting a line and any time you put the quilt away. The tape may damage the fabric if left on for a long period of time.*) To mark curved lines, carefully mark 1/4" from seam or appliqué at frequent intervals with a ruler. After a short amount of quilting experience, **Outline** quilting will feel more natural to you and marking these lines may not be necessary.

ORNAMENTAL

Quilting decorative lines or designs is called "Ornamental" quilting. Ornamental quilting is indicated on diagrams by dashed lines. This type of quilting should also be marked before you baste quilt layers together. To mark these lines follow the diagram and use quilting pattern included with each project. If your quilt top is light-colored, you may trace the quilting design directly onto the quilt top. If your quilt top is dark-colored, you may purchase a quilting stencil or make your own. To make stencil from whole pattern, place template plastic over quilting pattern and trace pattern onto plastic. Use a craft knife to cut slots approximately 1/8" wide along traced lines. To make stencils from half or quarter patterns, draw perpendicular lines in the center of a sheet of template plastic. Match center of quilting pattern to intersection of drawn lines on plastic. Trace half (or quarter) pattern onto plastic, turn template 1/2 or 1/4 turn; repeat until quilting pattern is complete. Use craft knife to cut slots approximately 1/8" wide along traced lines.

Refer to **Types of Quilting** to determine which quilting lines should be marked on your quilt top and mark the lines according to quilting diagrams.

PREPARING BACKING AND BATTING

The backing and batting should be a few inches larger on all sides than the quilt top to allow for the quilt top shifting slightly during quilting. Some fabrics, such as muslin, are available in 90" or 108" widths. Using 90" or 108" wide fabric will usually eliminate the need to piece the backing.

If you use a fabric that is not available in 90" or 108" widths, you will need to piece the backing. The backing should be pieced with the seams away from the center. This reduces the stress in the areas of the quilt that are folded most often.

To piece backing using 45"w fabric, cut fabric into two equal lengths. Matching right sides and long edges, pin fabric pieces together. Using a 1/2" seam allowance, sew pieces together along both long edges *(Fig. 39)*. Match seams (as when ironing pants) and press along one fold *(Fig. 40)*.

Fig. 39	Fig. 40

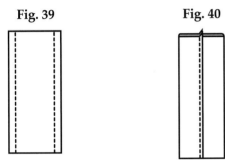

Cut along pressed fold, unfold fabric, and press seam allowances open *(Fig. 41)*.

Fig. 41

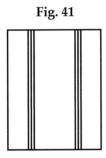

Cut batting same size as backing.

ASSEMBLING THE QUILT

Examine wrong side of quilt top closely and trim any seam allowances or clip any threads that may show through to the front of the quilt. Check quilting lines to make sure that all necessary lines have been marked.

Place backing fabric **wrong** side up on a flat surface. Tape or clip backing fabric to surface. Place batting on wrong side of backing fabric. Smooth batting, being sure to handle batting gently so as not to tear it. Center quilt top **right** side up on batting. Pin all layers together, placing pins approximately 4" apart and smoothing out bulges or wrinkles. Beginning each line of basting in the center and working toward the edges, use very long stitches to baste all layers together as shown in **Fig. 42**. *(Note: A spoon is very helpful for catching the tip of the needle on the quilt top when basting.)* Basting lines should be about 3-4" apart, with outer basting lines 1/2" from edges of quilt top.

Fig. 42

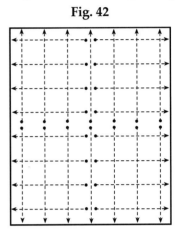

QUILTING

Secure center of quilt in hoop. Check quilt top and backing to make sure they are smooth.

The **Quilting Stitch** is a basic Running Stitch that forms a broken line on quilt top and backing. Stitches on quilt top and backing should be equal in length. Thread quilting needle with an 18-20″ length of quilting thread; a longer length may tangle or fray. Do not double thread; make a small knot in one end. Beginning in the center of the quilt, insert needle into quilt top and batting approximately ¹/₂″ from where you wish to begin quilting. Bring needle up at the point where you wish to begin *(Fig. 43)*; when knot catches on quilt top, give thread a quick, short pull to pop knot through fabric into batting *(Fig. 44)*.

Fig. 43   **Fig. 44**

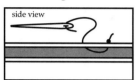 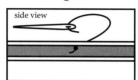

Holding the needle with your sewing hand and placing your other hand underneath the fabric, take the tip of the needle down through all layers. (**Note:** *Right-handers work from top to bottom or right to left. Left-handers work from top to bottom or left to right.*) As soon as needle touches your underneath finger, use that finger to push only the tip of the needle back up through layers. (**Note:** *The amount of the needle showing above the fabric determines the length of the quilting stitch. We recommend that beginners take 5-7 stitches per inch.*) Rocking the needle up and down, take 3-6 stitches before bringing the needle and thread completely through the layers *(Fig. 45)*. Check the back of the quilt to make sure stitches are going through all layers. If you are quilting through a seam allowance or quilting a curve or corner, you may need to take one stitch at a time.

Fig. 45

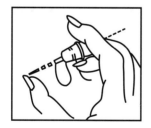

When you reach the end of your thread, tie a small knot close to the fabric and pop knot into batting; clip thread close to fabric. As in hand piecing, try to keep stitches straight and even. With practice, stitches will also be small.

It is very important to quilt from the center of the quilt out. If you try to quilt one side of the quilt and then the other, or quilt one block and then skip over to another block, you will find it hard to keep the quilt from puckering. Stop and move your hoop as often as necessary. You do not have to tie a knot every time you move your hoop; you may leave the thread dangling and pick it back up when you reach that part of the quilt again.

When you have finished quilting, remove all basting threads except those that are ¹/₂″ from edges of quilt top; these will secure the edges of the quilt while the binding is being attached. Trim batting and backing even with quilt top.

MAKING CONTINUOUS BIAS STRIP BINDING

Binding may be purchased, but making your own binding allows you to coordinate your binding color with the colors in your quilt.

1. Cut a square from binding fabric. (**Note:** *The required size square is noted in each project.*) Fold square in half diagonally; cut on fold to make two triangles.
2. With right sides together and using a ¹/₄″ seam allowance, sew triangles together *(Fig. 46)*; press seam allowances open.

Fig. 46

3. On wrong side of fabric, draw lines parallel to the long edges, the width specified in the project *(Fig. 47)*. Cut off any remaining fabric less than this width.

Fig. 47

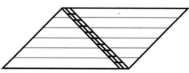

4. With right sides inside, bring short edges together to form a tube *(Fig. 48)*.

Fig. 48

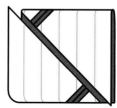

5. Match raw edges so that first line of top section meets second line of bottom section. Insert pins through drawn lines at the point where drawn lines intersect and make sure the pins go through intersections on both sides *(Fig. 49)*. Carefully pin edges together. Using a ¹/₄″ seam allowance, sew edges together.

Fig. 49

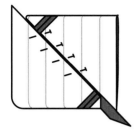

6. To cut continuous strip, begin cutting along first drawn line *(Fig. 50)*. Continue cutting along drawn line around tube.

Fig. 50

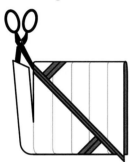

7. Trim each end of bias strip as shown in **Fig. 51**.

Fig. 51

8. Matching wrong sides and long edges, fold strip in half. Wrap binding around a piece of cardboard until ready to use.

ATTACHING BINDING WITH MITERED CORNERS

1. Fold one end of binding diagonally; press *(Fig. 52)*.

Fig. 52

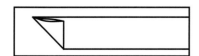

2. Matching raw edges and beginning with pressed end approximately 20″ from a corner, pin binding to right side of quilt along one side. Lay binding around quilt to make sure that seams in binding will not end up at a corner. Adjust binding if necessary.

3. When you reach the first corner, use your marking tool to mark ¹/₄″ from corner of quilt top *(Fig. 53)*.

Fig. 53

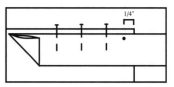

4. Using a ¹/₄″ seam allowance, sew binding to quilt top, backstitching at beginning of stitching and when you reach the mark *(Fig. 54)*. Lift needle out of fabric and clip thread.

Fig. 54

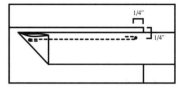

5. Fold binding as shown in **Figs. 55** and **56** and pin binding to adjacent side, matching raw edges. When you reach the next corner, use marking tool to mark ¹/₄″ from edge of quilt top.

Fig. 55   **Fig. 56**

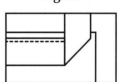 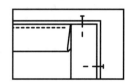

6. Backstitching at edge of quilt top, sew binding to quilt top *(Fig. 57)*; backstitch when you reach the mark. Lift needle out of fabric and clip thread.

Fig. 57

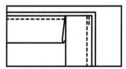

7. Repeat **Steps 5-6** to continue sewing binding to quilt top. Leaving a 2″ overlap, trim off excess binding. Stitch overlap in place.

8. On one edge of quilt, fold binding over to quilt backing and pin pressed edge in place, covering stitching line *(Fig. 58)*. On adjacent side, fold binding over, forming a mitered corner *(Fig. 59)*. Repeat to pin remainder of binding in place.

Fig. 58   **Fig. 59**

 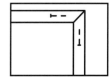

9. Blind stitch binding to backing.

MAKING A HANGING SLEEVE

You may wish to display your quilt by hanging it on a wall. Adding a hanging sleeve to the back of a quilt allows you to hang the quilt without distorting it.

1. Measure the width of the quilt, less 1". Cut a piece of fabric 3" wide by the determined measurement.
2. Press all edges 1/4" to wrong side; press edges 1/4" to wrong side again.
3. Machine stitch pressed edges in place.
4. With one long edge of hanging sleeve just below edge of binding or top of quilt, center and pin hanging sleeve to backing. Whipstitch long edges of hanging sleeve to backing.
5. Insert dowel into hanging sleeve.

SIGNING AND DATING YOUR QUILT

Signing and dating your quilt is a very important step in quilt making. It will let future generations know who made the quilt and when it was made. You may wish to add other personal information. Was the quilt made in honor of a special occasion, such as a wedding or the birth of a baby? Was the quilt made as a gift? The personalizing is basically writing your information on a small piece of fabric and appliquéing it to the backing.

1. Cut a 10" square of fabric and 9" square of freezer paper.
2. Center freezer paper shiny side down on wrong side of fabric. Iron freezer paper to fabric to stabilize fabric, holding iron on freezer paper 3-5 seconds. (*Note: Do not leave iron on freezer paper longer than 5 seconds, as it may make freezer paper difficult to remove from fabric.*)
3. If you wish to write your information inside a shape such as a heart or flower, make a template for the shape and draw around template on right side of fabric.
4. Use a permanent fine point marker to write the information inside drawn line. If desired, add a drawn design.
5. Remove freezer paper from back of fabric and trim fabric to 3/16" outside drawn line.
6. Position shape on back of quilt and appliqué shape to quilt, being careful to stitch through backing only.

MAKING PILLOWS

Any quilt block may be made into a pillow. If desired, you may add a ruffle and/or cording to the pillow top before adding the backing.

1. For pillow top, piece desired quilt block, referring to **General Instructions** as necessary.
2. Follow **Marking Quilting Lines**, pg. 154, to mark quilting lines.
3. For pillow top backing, cut a piece of fabric and a piece of fleece 3" larger on each side than pillow top. Follow **Preparing Backing and Batting**, pg. 155, to baste pillow top, fleece, and pillow top backing together.
4. Follow **Quilting**, pg. 156, to quilt pillow top. Trim fleece and backing even with pillow top.
5. For pillow backing, cut a square of fabric same size as pillow top.
6. To make cording, measure outer dimensions of pillow top and add 2". Cut a bias strip of fabric 1 1/2" wide and determined length (strip may be pieced). Lay purchased 1/4" dia cord along center of strip on wrong side of fabric; fold strip over cord. With zipper foot, machine baste along length of strip close to cord.
7. Matching raw edges and beginning at bottom center, pin cording to right side of pillow top making a clip in seam allowance of cording at each corner. Ends of cording should overlap approximately 2"; pin overlapping end out of the way. Starting 2" from beginning end of cording and ending 4" from overlapping end, baste cording to pillow top. On overlapping end of cording, remove 2 1/2" of basting; fold end of fabric back and trim cord so that it meets beginning end of cord. Fold end of fabric under 1/2"; wrap fabric over beginning end of cording. Finish basting cording to pillow top.
8. To make a ruffle, cut a strip of fabric twice desired finished width plus 1/2" for seam allowances and twice outer dimension of pillow top (measure pillow top on all four sides; then double measurement). Ruffle strip may be pieced. Press short ends 1/2" to wrong side. Fold strip in half lengthwise with wrong sides together and press. Baste 1/4" and 1/8" from raw edges. Pull basting threads, drawing up gathers to fit pillow top.
9. Start at bottom edge of pillow top and 1" from end of ruffle. Baste ruffle to right side of pillow top with finished edges toward center of pillow top and raw edges facing outward. Clip seam allowances at corners.
10. Hand stitch ends of ruffle together.
11. With right sides together, sew pillow backing to pillow top, leaving an opening at bottom edge. Turn right side out, carefully pushing corners outward. Stuff with polyester fiberfill and sew final closure by hand.

STITCH DIAGRAMS

(*Note:* *Number of strands of embroidery floss to use is included in individual projects.*)

BLANKET STITCH

Knot one end of floss. Bring needle up from wrong side of fabric at 1, even with edge of appliqué. Go down into appliqué at 2 and come up at 3, keeping floss below point of needle (*Fig. 60*). Continue to stitch in this manner, keeping stitches even (*Fig. 61*). Stitches should be approximately 3/16" long and 1/4" apart. Blanket stitches can also be worked around garment details, such as cuffs, collar edges, and lapels.

Fig. 60   **Fig. 61**

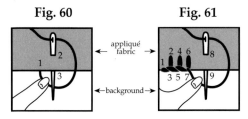

FEATHER STITCH

Knot 1 end of floss. Bring needle up from wrong side of fabric at 1. Go down into fabric at 2 and come up at 3, keeping floss below point of needle (*Fig. 62*). Alternate stitches from right to left, keeping stitches symmetrical (*Fig. 63*).

Fig. 62   **Fig. 63**

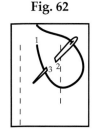

FRENCH KNOT

Knot 1 end of floss. Bring needle up from wrong side of fabric at 1. Wrap floss once around needle and insert needle at 2, holding end of floss with non-stitching fingers (*Fig. 64*). Tighten knot; then pull needle through, holding floss until it must be released. For larger knot, use more strands; wrap only once.

Fig. 64

LAZY DAISY STITCH

Knot 1 end of floss. Bring needle up from wrong side of fabric at 1 and make a loop. Go down at 1 and come up at 2, keeping floss below point of needle (*Fig. 65*). Pull needle through and go down at 3 to anchor loop, completing stitch.

Fig. 65

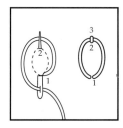

OUTLINE STITCH

Knot one end of floss. Bring needle up from wrong side of fabric at 1. With thumb holding floss above stitches, go down at 2 and come up at 3; pull needle through. Go down at 4 and up at 5 (same hole as 2), as shown in **Fig. 66**, keeping floss above stitches. Continue to stitch in this manner, keeping stitches even.

Fig. 66

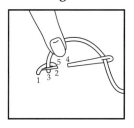

SATIN STITCH

Knot one end of floss. Bring needle up from wrong side of fabric at 1. Go down at 2 and come up at 3. Continue until area is filled (*Fig. 67*).

Fig. 67

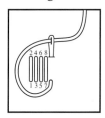

STRAIGHT STITCH

Knot 1 end of floss. Bring needle up from wrong side of block at 1 and go down at 2 (*Fig. 68*). Stitch lengths may be varied as desired. Stitches may be slanted as desired.

Fig. 68

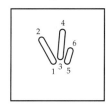

CREDITS

We want to extend a warm *thank you* to the generous people who allowed us to photograph our projects at their homes:

- *Burgoyne Surrounded*: Nancy Gunn Porter
- *Sawtooth Collection*: John and Anne Childs
- *Basket Collection*: Carol Clawson
- *Star of the Orient*: Dennis and Trisha Hendrix
- *Neighborly Collection*: Joan Gould
- *Baby Quilts*: Carol Clawson
- *Churn Dash Collection*: Nancy Gunn Porter
- *Pretty Pillows*: Carol Clawson
- *Quilt Block Sampler*: Christina Tiano
- *New York Beauty*: Dan and Sandra Cook
- *Bear's Paw Collection*: John and Anne Childs
- *Album Quilt*: John and Anne Childs
- *Sunny Garden*: Nancy Gunn Porter
- *Mariner's Compass*: Tom and Garrie Salmon
- *Pinwheel Quilt*: Nancy Gunn Porter

To Magna IV Color Imaging of Little Rock, Arkansas, we say thank you for the superb color reproduction and excellent pre-press preparation.

We want to especially thank photographers Mark Mathews, Ken West, Larry Pennington, and Karen Busick Shirey of Peerless Photography, Little Rock, Arkansas, and Jerry R. Davis of Jerry Davis Photography, Little Rock, Arkansas, for their time, patience, and excellent work.

To Donna Clark of The Santa Fe Trading Company, Little Rock, Arkansas, we extend a word of thanks for the use of the twig bed shown on page 15.

The Mariner's Compass quilt shown on page 113 is from the collection of Bryce and Donna Hamilton, Minneapolis, Minnesota.

We extend a sincere *thank you* to all the people who assisted in making and testing the projects in this book: Jennie Black, Frances Blackburn, Debbie Chance, Jane Douglas, Louella English, Marilyn Fendley, Wanda Fite, Nan Goode, Bonnie Gowan, Juanita Hodges, Minnie Hogan, Ida Johnson, Ruby Johnson, Richadeen Lewis, Velrie Louks, Gazelle Mode, Karen Tyler, Della Walters, and Minnie Whitehurst.